101 COOL PRACTICAL JOKES

with Glen Singleton

PRRR

HB

HINKLER
BOOKS

Cover Illustration and Illustrations: Glen Singleton
Cover Design: Hinkler Books Studio
Written by Nicolas Brasch
Editorial: Julie Haydon
Typesetting: Midland Typesetters, Maryborough, VIC, Australia

101 Cool Practical Jokes
Published in 2005 by Hinkler Books Pty Ltd
17–23 Redwood Drive
Dingley VIC 3172 Australia
www.hinklerbooks.com

ISBN: 1 7415 7232 0
Printed and bound in China

CONTENTS

Introduction

Playing practical jokes is great fun. Part of the fun comes from planning the joke and thinking about the end result. The rest of the fun comes from seeing the joke work. For a practical joke to work, there has to be a victim. The victim is the person the practical joke is played on. Some practical jokes have more than one victim. Whenever you carry out a practical joke, remember these two important rules:

- Practical jokes should never hurt anyone.
- Practical jokes should never be cruel.

This book contains 101 cool practical jokes. Each joke is divided into two main sections: the Sting and the Set-up. The Sting describes what happens to the victim in the joke. When a practical joke is successfully played on someone, it is said they have been 'stung'. The Set-up explains how to set-up and carry out the joke.

Some jokes also have sections called What You Need, Set-up Tips, Similar Jokes and Follow-up. What You Need gives details about all the items you need to carry out the trick. Set-up Tips gives a few extra hints about how to make the joke work. Similar Jokes describes jokes that are very similar to the one being described. Follow-up describes how you can add to the joke, sometimes days later, to make it even better.

Remember when playing a practical joke that a victim often seeks revenge. Don't play practical jokes unless you are willing to take them as well.

Just one more tip before you start. Never play a practical joke on someone who you know will not take it in good spirit. Practical jokes are meant to be fun.

4

Famous Practical Jokes

Over the past few hundred years, many practical jokes have become very well known. Some of the best jokes ever played include:

- A British television show convinced viewers that spaghetti grew on spaghetti trees (1957).

- An American sports magazine claimed that the New York Mets baseball team was trying to sign up a new pitcher who could throw a ball much faster than anyone had ever thrown one before. The problem was that the pitcher could not decide whether he wanted to play baseball or play the French horn (1985).

- The British businessman Richard Branson flew a hot-air balloon that looked like a flying saucer over London (1989).

- An American newspaper claimed that the Wisconsin State Capitol Building had collapsed after several explosions. The newspaper included a picture of the building with its dome falling off. This was in 1933, long before computers could fake photographs.

Quick and Easy Jokes

Here are a few quick and easy practical jokes. They require little preparation, use simple props and are over very quickly. Try some of these before going on to more complicated jokes.

Number 1: No Joke

This practical joke involves not playing a practical joke, which makes it a very good practical joke indeed. Does that make sense?

The Sting

It is traditional to play practical jokes on people on 1 April—April's Fool Day. April Fool's Day is approaching. Every year, you have played a practical joke on a particular victim. This year, the victim again expects to have a practical joke played on them. You remind them that April Fool's Day is approaching and they start getting worried. On the morning of April Fool's Day, they wake up in a sweat, dreading what's going to happen today. Until midday, when April Fool's Day officially ends, they cannot relax for a second. When midday passes, they breathe a big sigh of relief because they haven't been a victim of a practical joke. At least that's what they think. The fact that you didn't play a practical joke was a joke in itself because you had them so worried.

What You Need

- nothing, just a victim

The Set-up

1. As April Fool's Day approaches, pick a victim who would expect you to play a joke on them.

2. Every day, remind them how many days it is until April Fool's Day.

3. Tell them that you have a really big practical joke planned for them this year.

4. The day before April Fool's Day, walk past them rubbing your hands together, as if you are getting really excited about the joke you are going to play the following day.

5. On the morning of April Fool's Day, walk past them several times and chuckle or give them a grin. This will make them feel even more uncomfortable.

6. At one minute to midday on Aprils Fool's Day, walk up to the victim and say 'April Fool'.

7. When the victim reminds you that April Fool's Day ends in one minute and that you have not played a joke on them, tell them that you've been playing the joke all morning. Explain that the joke was the fact you didn't play a joke, but you still managed to have them running scared.

Number 2:
Kiss the Magic Ring

This joke relies on the victim believing that something wonderful will happen to them if they kiss a magic ring. It's up to you to convince the victim to have a go.

The Sting

The victim of the joke thinks they will be granted a special wish if they kiss a magic ring on your finger. Instead, they get a mouthful of lemon. What a sour joke!

What You Need

- an interesting ring

- a blindfold

- a lemon, cut into quarters

- a piece of string or an elastic band

The Set-up

1. Show the victim a ring on your finger. Tell them that the ring has been in your family for hundreds of years and that it is a magic ring.

2. Tell your victim that if they make a secret wish and then kiss the ring while blindfolded, their wish will be granted.

3. Once they've agreed to give it a try, blindfold them.

4. Tell them to think of a wish while you say some magic words.

5. Make up some magic-sounding words . While you are saying them, swap the ring with a lemon quarter tied to a piece of string or an elastic band.

6. When the lemon is in place on your finger, tell your

victim to lean towards the ring. Position your finger so that they kiss the lemon. They'll get the surprise of their life.

Set-up Tips

- Your victim may need some convincing to be blindfolded and kiss the ring. To help convince them, make up a tale about how someone in your family was helped by kissing the magic ring.

- Make sure that the piece of lemon is hidden from view before you blindfold your victim. Otherwise, they may guess what you are going to do.

Lemon

Number 3:
The Disappearing Money

Everyone loves finding money in the street. Particularly when the money is a note. This joke gets people excited about finding money. The problem is, they can't grab hold of it.

The Sting

The victim of the joke is walking down the street. They notice a piece of paper in the middle of the footpath. It looks like money but they can't be sure from a distance. As they get closer, they realise that they're right. They can't believe their luck. They think about what they're going to buy with the money. They bend down to pick it up. Just before they grab it, it skips away. Even if they chase the money, it keeps skipping away every time they get close to it.

What You Need

- a money note

- some fishing line

- a large bush, tree, fence or wall to hide behind

The Set-up

1. Make a tiny hole in the note and thread some fishing line through it.

2. Pick a place where there is a bush, tree, fence or wall that you can hide behind. Make sure that you have a good view of the footpath, but that people walking along the footpath cannot see you.

That's mine! I could buy a new sweater with that!

That's mine! You could buy me ten packs of dog chow with that!!

Ahhrr... it's a trick! I live on this footpath.. I see this one all the time!

3. When no one is coming, place the note on the footpath, then hide.

4. Hold the end of the fishing line and wait for a victim.

5. When someone bends down to pick up your note, jerk the fishing line so that the note moves away from the victim.

6. Keep doing this for as long as the person chases the note.

Set-up Tip

• You have to be very alert while you're doing this joke. Otherwise you may lose your money. Apart from running the risk of someone picking the note up before you have time to jerk the fishing line, you have to watch out for people using a foot to trap the money. If they stamp on the note before you pull the line, the note will stay under their shoe. Then you'll be the victim.

Similar Joke

• A similar joke can be done with a coin. Instead of using fishing line, use extra-strength glue to stick the coin to the footpath. Then stand back and watch people struggle to pick it free. The only problem with this joke is that you won't get your coin back.

Number 4:
A-tissue, A-tissue

This joke is a little bit like the magician's trick where the magician pulls a hanky out of a sleeve and ends up pulling out hanky after hanky, all tied to each other.

The Sting

The victim of the joke has a cold. They can feel a big sneeze building. They run to the box of tissues and pull the top one out. However, it is not just the top tissue that comes out. The second tissue comes out as well. And the third, and the fourth, and the fifth. In fact, every tissue comes out because for some reason they are all attached to each other. By this time, the victim has sneezed about ten times and they're in a real state, surrounded by tissues.

What You Need

- a box of tissues

- some glue

- someone with a cold

- about half an hour without interruption

The Set-up

1. Open the box of tissues and take out every single tissue. (The easiest way to get the tissues out is by opening the box at the bottom.) Make sure that you keep the tissues folded up. Otherwise they will be very hard to put back into the tissue box.

2. Take the bottom edge of the top tissue and glue it to the top edge of the second tissue.

3. Take the bottom edge of the second tissue and glue it to the top edge of the third tissue.

4. Repeat this process until you have glued the second last tissue to the last tissue.

5. Place the tissues back in the box, with the top edge of the top tissue poking out of the top of the box.

6. Tape or glue the bottom of the box so that the tissues won't fall out.

7. Place the box where it can be easily seen and reached. Then stand back and watch the fun.

Number 5: Buzzing Balloons

If you blow up a balloon and tie a knot in the end, you have something you can kick and hit. If you blow up a balloon and don't tie a knot in the end, you have something that can whiz and buzz around a room.

The Sting

The victim of the joke is about to walk into a room. Everything seems normal and they do not suspect that they are about to have a practical joke played on them. All that changes as they turn the doorknob and open the door. As the door opens, a balloon whizzes around the room, giving the victim a nasty scare. They have no idea where the balloon came from. And if you don't tell them, they never will know.

What You Need

- a balloon

- a door and doorframe

The Set-up

1. Blow up a balloon. Do not tie a knot in the end of the balloon.

2. Place the end of the balloon between the door and the doorframe, so that the balloon is held in place and is not losing air. You may have to try various doors and

doorframes before you find a suitable one.

3. Close the door and wait for your victim to open the door.

4. If you want to make a really big impact, place a few balloons in the door. The more you have, the bigger the buzz.

5. Stand back and watch the look on your victim's face as they open the door and the balloon you positioned between the door and doorframe is suddenly released. It will start to whiz about. Your victim won't be able to work out what's going on.

Similar Jokes

- Place a bucket of water on top of a slightly open door. Make sure that the bucket is fastened to something so that it tips when the door opens, but does not fall. You do not want a full bucket of water dropping on someone's head.

- Place a bag full of flour on top of a slightly open door. When the victim opens the door, the bag will fall on their head, causing a great mess. Make sure the bag is not too heavy. You don't want to knock anyone out.

- Balance a row of ping-pong balls along the top of a slightly open door. When the victim pushes the door, the balls will fall all over the place.

Number 6: Holding the String

You can play this joke on one or two people. Either way, it's fun. The length of the joke depends on how long it takes before the victim realises they have been the target of a practical joker.

The Sting

The victim is walking along the footpath. You are standing nearby with a ball of string, a ruler and other measuring equipment. You are looking rather flustered. As the victim passes, you approach them and ask if they would mind holding one end of the string for a minute while you take the other end around the corner to do some measuring. The victim agrees. They stand still, holding the string. They wait for a couple of minutes and you have not returned. They are getting impatient, but they keep holding the string for a bit longer. Finally, they have had enough and they go looking for you. They turn the corner and you are nowhere to be seen.

What You Need

- a ball of string
- some measuring equipment
- a corner block

The Set-up

1. Set up your equipment on a corner block. You have to make sure that the person you ask to hold the string will not be able to see around the corner.

2. Other than the ball of string, it doesn't really matter what your other measuring equipment is. It's only there for show, to look as if you are doing some serious measuring.

3. When your victim approaches, ask them if they could help you for a minute. Tell them that you are doing a school project and that you have to measure from the point where they are standing to another point just around the corner.

4. Pick up your measuring equipment and take the other end of the string around the corner, where the victim can no longer see you.

5. Tie the end of the string to a fence or gate. If you want to fool another person, ask someone else to hold the end of the string and tell them that you have to check a measurement around the next corner.

6. Leave the scene. You can go home and wonder how long the victim or victims waited, or you can hide somewhere and watch how long it takes them to realise they have been stung.

Number 7: CD Swap

This joke will frustrate your victim. It is especially good to play this joke on people who are particular about the way they organise their CD collection.

The Sting

The victim goes to put on one of their favourite CDs. They turn the CD player on, take the CD out of its cover and put it in the player. They press the 'Play' button and get a shock when the music that plays is not what they expected. They take the CD out and check the label. It does not match the cover. They grab another CD from their collection and look inside. This one is also wrong. They go through their entire collection and every single CD has been swapped around.

What You Need

- the victim's CD collection
- about half an hour to do the swapping

The Set-up

1. Make sure the victim is occupied elsewhere for at least half an hour.

2. Stack the CD covers into one large pile. Do not take the CDs out of their covers yet.

3. Open the top CD cover and take the CD out. Open the second CD cover and take the CD out. Place the first CD into the second CD cover.

4. Open the third CD cover and take the CD out. Place the second CD into the third CD cover.

5. Repeat this process right to the bottom of the pile. The last CD will go in the top CD cover. (The reason for swapping the CDs in such an organised manner is to ensure that no CD is put back into its own cover.)

6. Put the CDs back where you got them from. If the victim always has their CDs in a certain order, make sure that you put them back in the same order. Otherwise they'll suspect someone has touched them.

Similar Jokes

- You can also play this joke with people's video collections and vinyl record collections.

- You can swap people's books around by swapping the dust covers on their books. To make things even worse for the victim, put some of the dust covers on upside down.

Number 8: CD Replacement

This practical joke is similar to the CD Swap joke but gives the victim even more of a shock. Particularly when they hear a song that they can't stand.

The Sting

The victim goes to put on one of their favourite CDs. They turn the CD player on, take the CD out of its cover and put it in the player. They press the 'Play' button and get a shock when the music that plays is not what they expected. They wanted to play Powderfinger but ended up hearing Frank Sinatra. They check some of their other CDs. Their Silverchair CD contains Dean Martin, and their Best of U2 CD is actually the Best of Tony Bennett. They go through their entire collection and every single CD is wrong.

What You Need

- the victim's CD collection
- some cheap, second-hand CDs
- a box
- about half an hour to do the replacing

The Set-up

1. Go to a second-hand CD shop and buy some very cheap CDs that you know your victim will hate.

2. Make sure the victim is occupied elsewhere for at least half an hour.

3. Take the second-hand CDs out of their covers.

4. Take the victim's CDs out of their covers and put them into the covers from the second-hand CDs.

5. Put the second-hand CDs into the victim's CD covers.

6. Put the victim's CD covers back where you got them from.

7. Stack the second-hand CD covers into the box and store them somewhere safe. At some stage, you will give the CDs back to the victim. You can then use the second-hand CDs to play the same joke on someone else.

Follow-up

- A couple of days after playing this joke, send the victim one of their CDs through the post. Make sure that it is well wrapped and padded so it doesn't get ruined. Also include a ransom note offering to return their CDs in return for a gift. Tell them a time and place to leave the gift, as well as a time and place to pick up their CDs.

Number 9:
'Look, Up in the Sky'

This joke costs nothing, needs no equipment and can have many victims. That makes it a very good practical joke to play.

The Sting

A crowd of people is gathered at the bottom of a tall building. Everyone is looking up at the top of the building. Some of the people start whispering and asking each other what is going on. Over the next few minutes, the crowd grows bigger and bigger. Rumours start spreading that someone is out on the roof of the building. After about ten minutes, the crowd has become so large that it is holding up traffic. A police officer comes along and tells the crowd

to move away. Eventually, the crowd does move away. Many of them watch the television news that night to see if anything dramatic happened. Of course, the incident doesn't make it to the news because nothing did happen. It was all a practical joke started by you.

What You Need

- a tall building in a busy street
- a couple of volunteers

The Set-up

1. Pick a tall building in a busy street.

2. When there are quite a few people walking past, stand at the bottom of the building and look up at the top.

3. Have one of your friends walk past and stop near you. You have to act as if you don't know each other. Your friend should also look up.

4. Have another friend walk past and stop. Again, you should all act as if you don't know each other. One of you should point towards the top of the building and whisper something to the others.

5. By now, you should have aroused the interest of people passing by.

6. As the crowd of people grows, you and your friends should walk away and watch from somewhere else.

Similar Jokes

*   If you are on a crowded beach, look at the sea and point out into the distance.

*   If you are at a sporting event, stand up and look at a point several rows behind you.

*   If you are in the classroom, look out of the window and point into the distance.

Number 10: Cool Confetti

In this joke, confetti rains on people when they are inside a room. It can only be played on hot days when people are seeking a little cool relief. Your classroom would be a great place to play the Cool Confetti practical joke.

The Sting

In a classroom, children are waiting for their teacher to arrive. The children are yelling loudly and running around. It is a warm day and everyone is getting a bit hot. The teacher arrives and tells everyone to be quiet and to sit in their seats. The teacher notices that the overhead fan is not on, so the teacher switches it on. The blades of the fan slowly start to spin around. As the speed of the blades increases, confetti starts to rain down on everyone. The schoolchildren scream with delight, and the teacher can do nothing but watch as more and more colourful confetti falls from the blades and is blown about the room by the draught made by the fan.

What You Need

- a room with an overhead, spinning fan

- confetti

- a stepladder or desk and chair

- someone to help

The Set-up

1. Make sure that it is a hot day. If you play this trick in the middle of winter, you'll be waiting months before anyone turns the fan on.

2. Pick a room where there is an overhead fan with wide blades.

3. Make sure the fan is turned off.

4. Climb to the top of the stepladder or place a chair on top of a table and carefully climb onto the chair.

5. Get someone to hold the stepladder or chair for you. They should also make sure that no one walks into the room and turns the fan on.

6. Pour the confetti on top of the fan blades and spread it around.

7. Get down and hide the stepladder or put the table and chair back in place.

8. Wait for someone to turn the fan on, then watch as it starts raining confetti.

Similar Jokes

You don't have to put confetti on top of the fan blades. There are other items you can use. Here are a few suggestions:

- rice

- toy plastic flies or plastic spiders (to give people a fright)

- plastic bags or tiny cups full of water (to make it seem like it's really raining)

Whatever you use, make sure that it won't hurt anyone when it falls from the fan.

Number 11: Making an Impression

This practical joke leaves quite a mark on your victim! And sometimes the victim can walk around for ages before realising they've been stung.

The Sting

You and the victim are playing a game with some coins. You persuade the victim to try and stick a coin to their forehead. They do so. When they take the coin away, they are left with a dark impression of the coin. Even though everyone else can see the impression of the coin, the victim is unaware that they have been stung.

What You Need

- two coins
- a felt pen or some powder

The Set-up

1. Fill in one side of a coin with the felt pen or cover it with powder. Make-up powder is very good for this purpose.

2. Stand in front of your victim and press the coin that is not marked onto your forehead.

3. When your victim asks what you are doing, tell them that you heard on the radio that people who can stick coins to their forehead are supposed to be smarter than those who can't. Your victim will probably want to have a go, so that they can prove how smart they are.

4. Tell the victim that you'll show them exactly where the

There's always one in every crowd

If you can get a coin to stick to your forehead it means you're smart... What does it mean if you can get a whole handbag full of loose change to stick?

coin has to go. Take the coin that has the marked side and press that side firmly in the middle of the victim's forehead. Make sure the victim does not see the marks or powder.

5. Tell the victim to hold the coin firmly in place for two minutes. After two minutes, tell the victim to let go.

6. If the coin is stuck to the forehead, pull the coin off and tell them that they are obviously very intelligent.

7. If the coin falls off, grab it and put it in your pocket. Tell them that you couldn't make the coin stick either. This will make them feel better.

8. Whether the coin sticks or falls, the victim will have an impression of the coin stuck on their forehead and they will walk around without realising it.

Number 12: Name That Tune

Some tunes are nice to hear once or twice. After a few hearings, they can begin to get on your nerves. After many, many hearings they start to drive you mad. This practical joke drives people mad.

The Sting

The victim is sitting in the lounge relaxing. They are reading a book and do not want to be disturbed. Suddenly, they hear a tune. They ignore it, hoping it will go away. A few minutes later, they notice the tune is still playing. Now they are having trouble concentrating on their book and they are not as relaxed as they were. After ten minutes, they get up to find where the tune is coming from. It seems to be coming from inside a cupboard. They open the cupboard door and begin to rummage through the contents. The tune is still playing. Finally, at the back of the cupboard, they discover a small device playing the tune. By now, the floor is full of stuff they have thrown out of the cupboard and they are feeling anything but relaxed.

What You Need

- a musical birthday card

- a room with a hiding place

The Set-up

1. Buy a musical birthday card.

2. Take the musical chip out of the card.

3. Pick a hiding place, such as a cupboard, in your classroom, at home, or in an office or store. Make sure the hiding place is near where the victim sits.

4. When you know the victim is on their way, set the musical chip off and put it in the hiding place.

5. Leave the scene.

Similar Joke

• While going on a long family holiday in the car, set a musical chip off and put it down the back of a seat or somewhere else it cannot easily be reached. It will drive everyone mad (though it might drive you mad as well).

29

Number 13: Hat Trick

The Hat Trick joke makes the victim feel more foolish than just about any other joke in this book. And it's so simple.

The Sting

The victim is walking down the street wearing a cap, minding their own business. Suddenly, they feel someone touch the top of their head and run away, carrying what appears to be the victim's cap. The victim begins chasing the thief. The chase goes on for some time before the victim catches the thief. The victim tries to grab the cap but the thief holds onto it tightly. The victim tells the thief to give them the cap back, but the thief claims that the cap belongs to them. When the victim argues, the thief points to the victim's head. The victim touches their head to find that their cap is still there.

Hey! Come back with my NERDS AGAINST GENETICALLY ENGINEERED SOYBEANS cap!

KEEP THE BEANS FREE

What You Need

- a victim with a cap

- a cap identical to the victim's cap

The Set-up

1. Choose a victim who has a distinctive-looking cap.

2. Borrow or buy a cap that is identical to the victim's cap.

3. Follow the victim as they walk down a long street.

4. Run up to the victim, pretend to grab their cap, then run in front of them waving your cap. The victim will probably think that the cap you are holding is their cap.

5. If the victim chases you, let them eventually catch you.

If they don't chase you, tease them by waving the cap in front of them. They will eventually try to get you.

6. When the victim grabs you, pretend you don't know why they have grabbed you.

7. When the victim claims that the cap belongs to them, point to their head and tell them that they're still wearing their cap.

Number 14: Splash

In this joke, the poor victim gets stung simply because they are trying to help you. Next time they are about to do a good deed, they might think twice.

The Sting

The victim believes you are going to do a trick involving nailing a glass of water to the wall. Of course, they do not believe you can succeed and they want to watch you fail. When you drop the nail, they bend down to pick it up. They're just doing you a favour. But they get a big shock when the glass of water is tipped over their head.

What You Need

- a glass
- water
- a wall
- a nail
- a hammer

OOOPS! I'm just so clumsy!

The Set-up

1. Fill a glass with water. It is important that you use a glass and not a plastic or paper cup.

2. Tell the victim that you are going to nail the glass of water to a wall. The victim will not believe you can succeed and will be keen to watch you fail.

3. Ask the victim to hold the hammer for you. (This gets them used to helping you.)

4. Place the glass against the wall.

5. Begin to put the nail in place, then drop the nail to the floor beneath the glass.

6. Ask the victim to pick the nail up for you because you cannot let go of the glass.

7. When the victim is under the glass, tip the glass upside down so that the water falls onto their head.

Number 15: Baby Face

Everyone has photos of themselves as babies. Most people do not want these photos seen by their friends. If you can get your hands on a friend's baby photos, you can cause a lot of embarrassment.

The Sting

The victim arrives at their school. Almost as soon as they walk through the front gates, other children are staring and laughing at them. The victim checks their clothes and hair but everything seems in place. They can't understand why people are pointing. When they walk past the main school block, the reason for the stares and laughs becomes obvious. Stuck to the wall are baby photos of the victim with the victim's name underneath. As the victim walks around school, they find more and more of their baby photos hanging up.

What You Need

- an original baby photo of the victim

- copies of the victim's baby photo

- sticky tape

The Set-up

1. Get hold of one of the victim's baby photos. You do not need the negatives of the photo to have copies made.

2. Scan the photo into a computer and print out lots of copies, or you could make photocopies of the photo.

3. Get to school early one morning, long before the victim turns up.

4. Stick the photos up all over the school.

5. There are many other places where you can stick up baby photos of your victim. Here are a few suggestions:

- at a shopping centre

- at a skateboard park

- on telephone poles around the neighbourhood

Number 16: Overflow

Keep a mop handy for this joke. The victim is going to need to use it to clean up.

The Sting

The victim goes to the toilet. Everything seems normal until they flush the toilet. Suddenly, soapsuds are overflowing from the toilet bowl. The soapsuds flow down the side of the toilet bowl and onto the floor. It is like a horror movie, with monster suds emerging from the sewer.

What You Need

- a bottle of detergent

- a toilet

The Set-up

1. Pour the entire contents of the detergent bottle into the toilet bowl.

2. Do not flush the toilet. It is the flush that sets the detergent off.

3. Wait for the victim to go to the toilet.

Similar Joke

- Toilets are not the only places where this joke works. You can put detergent in a fountain and watch the suds develop. However, never put detergent in a fountain that contains fish.

Not So Quick and Easy Jokes

Now you've tried some quick and easy jokes, here are a few that require a bit more time and effort. These jokes are probably more rewarding than the quick jokes because the longer you plan a joke and the harder you work to carry it out, the more satisfying it is when your victim is stung.

Number 17: Changing Room

Have you ever had the urge to move all the furniture in your bedroom, just for a change? Well, it's much more fun if you do it in a friend's room—without them knowing.

The Sting

The victim goes to their bedroom after being away for the day. They open the bedroom door and cannot believe their eyes. Their bed is where the desk usually is, and the desk is where the bed usually is. The posters that were on the walls are now on the ceiling, and the rug from the floor is hanging over the curtain rod. The clothes that were hanging in the wardrobe have been squashed into the chest of drawers, and the socks, underpants and handkerchiefs that were in the chest of drawers are now on hangers in the wardrobe.

What You Need

- a friend's bedroom
- some friends to help you
- about half a day

The Set-up

1. Get permission from the victim's parents to change the victim's bedroom around. (You will probably have to promise to help the victim put everything back where it was.)

2. Find out when the victim will be away from home for a few hours.

3. Make a plan at least a day before the joke. Draw a map of the victim's bedroom and work out where you are going to put everything.

4. Write down the order in which you are going to move things. This will make things much easier on the day.

5. On the day of the joke, start work as soon as the victim leaves home. You may need all the time you can get.

6. Make sure you have a few friends to help you lift and move the items around.

7. When you have finished, leave a note on the bed with a message for the victim to work out. It could be the name of a furniture-moving service made up of the first letters of everyone who helped play the joke.

Safety Tip

- Lifting heavy objects can cause injuries. When you lift anything heavy, make sure that you bend your knees and pick the object up from the bottom. This should help avoid painful back injuries.

Number 18:
Changing Room (Slowly)

This practical joke is similar to the Changing Room joke, except that small changes are made over a period of time. It is interesting to see how long it takes the victim to realise what is happening.

The Sting

The victim goes to their bedroom after a day at school. They throw their bag onto a chair, as they usually do. However, the bag misses the chair and falls to the floor. The victim has never missed before. The next night, the victim is lying in bed and goes to switch their bedside lamp on. They have to reach over a bit further than they normally do. On the weekend, they wake up looking forward to playing sport. They open their wardrobe door and reach for their sports uniform. It is not where it usually is. They eventually find it where their school uniform usually hangs. It takes two weeks before the victim realises they have been stung by a practical joke.

What You Need

- repeat access to a friend's bedroom

The Set-up

1. Let the victim's parents know what you plan to do and arrange a time when you can pop over and play the joke each day.

2. Every day or every couple of days, make a small change to the victim's room. Here are a few suggestions:

- move a chair a short distance

Hey... this isn't my dress... it's not the right size! And come to think of it... this isn't even my wardrobe!

- move the bed a short distance

- move the bedside lamp a short distance

- make one of the posters or pictures a little uneven

- move a couple of items of clothing from one drawer into another drawer

3. Do not make major changes or more than one change a day. The idea is to see how long the joke can last.

4. If the joke goes on for a long time and you want the victim to realise they have been stung, leave a note that gives them a clue as to what has been going on.

Similar Joke

- Rather than move items around, you could remove one small item a day from the victim's room. Keep them at home in a box until the victim says something, then hand them back. If the victim hasn't noticed anything missing after a week, take a large object, such as a chair.

Number 19:
Leaves, Leaves, Leaves

Have you ever wondered what to do with the piles of leaves that collect under trees? Well, here's one idea that will bring a smile to your face.

The Sting

The victim wakes up in the morning and gets ready for work. They have a shower, eat breakfast and say goodbye to their family. They open the front door and go to step outside. But they can't take a single step because they are faced with the largest pile of leaves they have seen in their life. They have to push and shove the leaves out of the way before they can make their way outside. At the end of the day, when they return home, they find their front door is again blocked by a huge pile of leaves. This time they can't get into their house without pushing the leaves away.

What You Need

- lots and lots of leaves
- garbage bags
- a chair or stepladder

The Set-up

1. Collect as many leaves as you can from your garden. You can even offer to rake up your neighbours' gardens so you can get more leaves.

2. Pack all the leaves into garbage bags.

3. Get up early before the victim is out of bed and take the garbage bags full of leaves to the victim's house. Empty one of the bags before the front door.

4. Empty a second bag on top of the pile, then empty a third bag and a fourth bag.

5. By now you will probably need the chair or stepladder to reach the top of the pile.

6. Hide somewhere so that you can see the reaction on the victim's face when they open the front door.

7. You could also do this joke while your victim is out during the day, or repeat it in the afternoon so they are stung twice.

Set-up Tip

- Do not attempt this joke when it is windy, otherwise the leaves will just blow away before the victim comes across the pile.

Similar Joke

- If you live in an area that gets hit by snowstorms in winter, you could shovel huge piles of snow instead of leaves.

Number 20: Holiday Snaps

This joke takes some organising but it is very funny. Some people use garden gnomes to play this joke, but you can use your victim's favourite toy or other item.

The Sting

The victim gets an envelope in the mail. They open it up and inside is a photograph of their favourite teddy bear at the airport. On the back of the photo is a note saying 'You never take me anywhere, so I've gone on a trip by myself'. The victim races up to their room to look for their teddy bear. They can't find it anywhere. Over the next few weeks, they receive lots of photos of their teddy bear at various holiday destinations. One morning, just as they begin to wonder whether they will ever see their teddy bear again, they open the front door to find their teddy bear on the doormat. The bear is holding a note saying 'I'm back. Did you miss me?'.

What You Need

- a toy or favourite item from the victim

- a camera

- envelopes

- stamps

- someone going on a holiday

The Set-up

1. Find someone who is going on a holiday and is willing to help you play this joke. If you are going on holiday, you can do it yourself, but the victim may guess that you're playing a practical joke on them. It is best if the victim does not know the person on holiday.

2. Sneak one of the victim's favourite toys out of their room. Don't worry, they will get it back. A doll, teddy bear or other soft toy is best.

3. Give the toy to the person going on holiday.

4. Also give the person going on holiday your victim's address and a few envelopes. If the person is having a holiday within your country, you can give them the stamps they'll need. If the person is going overseas, they will have to buy the stamps themselves. You can give them some money to pay for the stamps.

5. Instruct the person going on holiday to position the toy in front of famous landmarks and take photos of the toy.

6. They should then write a message on the back of each photo and send the photos to the victim.

7. When the person returns from holiday, get the toy back and place it outside the victim's front door.

OK Teddy.
Smile for the camera and say...
Here I am in London. Its a little chilly! Wish I'd packed a warm cardigan! Bet you wish you were here!

Number 21: Storm in a Bathroom

A public toilet is one place where people probably think they are safe from practical jokes. But you know better, don't you?

The Sting

The victim walks into a toilet stall in a public toilet. As soon as they have closed and locked the door, the lights flicker on and off and someone yells out 'Lightning, Lightning'. A moment later, they hear the sound of banging and someone yells out 'Thunder, Thunder'. They get ready to leave the stall but it's too late. Someone yells out 'Rain', and a moment later they are drenched after being hit by water coming over the top of the door.

What You Need

- a public toilet
- the light switch
- a bucket
- some water

The Set-up

1. Pick a public toilet.

2. Fill the bucket with water.

3. Wait until the victim goes in to a stall and closes the door.

4. Switch the lights on and off a number of times, then yell out 'Lightning, Lightning'.

5. Wait a moment, then run past the stalls, banging your fists on the doors and yelling 'Thunder, Thunder'.

6. Wait a moment, then pick the bucket up and carry it towards the victim's stall.

7. Yell out 'Rain, Rain', and throw the water over the top of the stall door.

8. Run as fast as you can. If the victim finds out who you are, you're likely to receive a drenching yourself.

Number 22: Glitter from Above

This joke requires a fair bit of setting up and testing but it's well worth the effort. It will take the victim ages to get rid of all the glitter that has fallen on them.

The Sting

The victim sits down at their desk to do a bit of homework. They get their books ready and take their pens and pencils out of their pencil case. Before starting, they decide to sharpen their pencils. They open the desk drawer where they keep their pencil sharpener. A moment  later, a pile of glitter falls from the ceiling and onto their head, their books and all over the carpet. What a mess!

What You Need

- a white handkerchief

- glitter or confetti

- fishing line

- pins or sticky tape

- a desk with a drawer

- a ladder

- a couple of hours to set up and test the joke

The Set-up

1. Make a small hole in the middle of one of the edges of the handkerchief.

2. Tie one end of the fishing line to the hole.

3. Fill the handkerchief with glitter.

4. Position the ladder so that you can reach the ceiling above the victim's desk chair.

5. Climb the ladder and lightly pin or tape the four corners of the handkerchief to the ceiling.

6. The fishing line will be dangling from the handkerchief. Lightly tape it in a couple of places so that it sticks to the ceiling and the wall. You do not want it dangling in view.

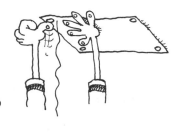

7. Tie the free end of the fishing line to the back of the top drawer of the desk.

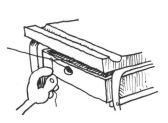

8. The victim opens the drawer, tugging on the fishing line. This pulls the handkerchief away from the ceiling. The glitter falls on the victim's head.

9. You will probably have to practise this a number of times to make sure that you have not attached the handkerchief too tightly to the ceiling.

Food and Drink Jokes

The jokes in this chapter involve food and drink. However, not every joke requires the victim to eat or drink. In some cases, food is used to look like other items.

Number 23: The Holey Cup

Watch the victim's frustration as they try their best to quench their thirst—only to end up with the contents of their drink down the front of their shirt.

The Sting

The victim of the joke gets ready to drink something delicious. Imagine how frustrated they get when the liquid leaks out of the cup and onto their clothes before it reaches their mouth.

What You Need

I would have enjoyed that drink... if my shirt hadn't drunk it all first!

- a plastic cup

- a pin

- a tasty drink

- a cloth

The Set-up

1. Use the pin to prick some holes just below the rim of the cup.

2. Tempt the victim with the offer of a tasty drink.

3. Pour the drink, but make sure that the liquid remains below the pinholes.

4. Give the victim the drink.

5. Watch as the drink spurts out of the holes before it can reach the victim's mouth.

What's delicious wet, cold...and all over somebody's shirt?

THIS DRINK!!

6. Use the cloth to help the victim clean themselves up.

Set-up Tips

- Make sure that the holes in the cup are large enough for liquid to flow through but small enough so that the victim cannot see them.

- Practise the joke with water before your victim is at your house. That way you can make sure the holes are exactly the right size.

- Know what your victim's favourite drink is. That way they'll find your offer of a drink hard to refuse.

Number 24:
The Holey Straw

This practical joke is similar to the Holey Cup joke, except that it is a straw that causes the problem.

The Sting

Like the Holey Cup joke, the victim of the joke gets ready to drink something delicious. This time, their frustration comes about because they cannot suck any liquid up through their straw. No matter how hard they suck on the straw, all that happens is their face gets redder and redder.

What You Need

- a straw

- a pin

- a cup or can of tasty drink

The Set-up

1. Use the pin to prick two holes near the bottom of the straw and two more near the top of the straw. The holes should be opposite each other.

2. Give the victim the drink. It is best if it is a drink that you know they like. That way they'll find it hard to refuse.

3. Watch as they try to suck the drink up through the straw. The holes make it virtually impossible for liquid to make its way up the straw.

4. Encourage the victim to suck harder. Then enjoy the discomfort they are experiencing.

Follow-up

- You could have a second holey straw handy. Then you could tell the victim that there must be something wrong with the first straw and offer them the replacement. Watch with delight as they struggle again.

Number 25:
The Knotty Straw

Here's another joke involving a straw. Like the Holey Straw joke, the victim will suck and suck and never get anywhere. For this joke to work, the victim has to have a cup with a lid on it, like the sort served in fast-food outlets.

The Sting

The victim of the joke eats some of their food and gets ready to take a drink. They start sucking on their straw but nothing happens. They suck harder and harder, still nothing comes out. Meanwhile, everyone at the table is laughing at the victim's attempts to have a drink.

What You Need

- a cup of drink—the cup must have a lid

- a straw

- a few seconds to prepare the joke

The Set-up

1. Next time you're at a fast-food outlet, pick out a friend to do the trick on.

2. Make sure that your friend buys a drink.

3. If they do not want a drink, offer to buy one for them. They'll find your offer hard to refuse.

4. Now you need to be alone with the drink for a few seconds. Offer to carry their drink to the table for them.

5. Get to the table as fast as you can and pull the lid off the drink. Take the straw out and tie a knot in the middle.

6. Put the straw and lid back before the victim gets to the table. The knot in the straw will stop any drink getting to their mouth.

7. If the victim insists on carrying their drink, wait until they go to the toilet or arrange for someone to distract them.

Number 26: The Goldfish

Play this joke on a friend who has a goldfish. It's amazing how much a carrot can look like a goldfish.

The Sting

The victim of the joke is very proud of their goldfish. Every time you go around to their house, they show it to you. This time, as they show it to you, you mention how hungry you are. The victim goes into the kitchen to find something to eat and you follow. They have their back turned to you, but they hear you mumble with your mouth full, 'It's too late. I couldn't help myself. I was just so hungry'. They turn and scream, as they see the tail of their goldfish hanging out the end of your mouth. You take one big gulp and the tail disappears as well.

What You Need

- a carrot

- a sharp knife

- a victim with a goldfish

My favourite goldfish...! You've eaten my favourite goldfish! You didn't eat my PIRANHA too did you?

The Set-up

1. Get a carrot.

2. Using the knife, carefully cut the ends off the carrot. Carve the thick part of the carrot in the shape of a goldfish tail. Make sure that you do not cut yourself with the knife. (You don't have to carve the carrot into the shape of a whole goldfish, as your victim will only see the piece hanging out of your mouth.)

3. Next time you go over to the victim's house put the carved carrot into your pocket.

4. When the victim shows you their goldfish, make a comment about how hungry you are.

5. If the victim does not show you their goldfish, ask to see it, then make a comment about how hungry you are.

OK ... I can carve a goldfish out of a carrot ... But what if he has a WHALE in his aquarium?

What do I carve that out of? A VERY VERY large turnip?

6. As you follow your victim into the kitchen, pull the carrot out of your pocket. Then place it in your mouth, with the tail piece hanging out.

7. Make a loud, mumbling comment about not being able to wait.

8. After you've chewed and swallowed the 'tail', say, 'Goldfish aren't nearly as bad as I thought they'd be'. Then ask, 'Have you got any more?'.

Number 27:
Sausage Fingers

This joke will scare the pants off the victim. They'll probably run to the phone to call an ambulance before they realise that it's a joke.

The Sting

The victim of the joke shakes your hand. They get the shock of their life when you pull your hand away and scream. They are left holding what they think is one of your fingers. It turns out to be a sausage.

What You Need

- a sausage (the colour of the sausage should be as close to that of your skin as possible)

- knife

- tomato sauce (optional)

How do you do young man? Is that a sausage with sauce on the end.. or is that... aahhrr... A FINGER THAT FELL OFF??

The Set-up

1. Buy a sausage that is very close to the colour of your skin. It should also be skinny.

2. Trim the sausage so that it is about the same length as one of your fingers. Be very careful when using a knife to trim the sausage.

3. Just before meeting the victim, place the sausage between two of your fingers.

4. As the victim approaches, get ready to greet them but don't put your hand out too soon. You don't want them seeing six fingers on your hand or they may get suspicious.

5. At the very last moment, put out your hand for them to shake.

6. Shake hands, then pull your hand away, leaving them holding the sausage. Then scream as though in pain.

Follow-up

- You can add to the joke by placing tomato sauce on the fingers that the sausage is between. The tomato sauce will look like blood.

Those big fat barbecue sausages look just like fingers. I'd like to try one on for size please! If it fits.. how much for just ONE?

Number 28: Smelly House

This joke takes a while to become effective, but once it does, it stinks! And one of the best parts of this joke is that by the time the victim realises they've been stung, you are long gone and they have no idea who played the joke on them.

The Sting

The victim does not notice anything is wrong, at first. However, over the next few days they notice a smell in their living room. They assume that the smell will go away, but it doesn't. It just gets worse. Finally, the smell gets so bad that the victim tries to find where it's coming from. They get down on their hands and knees and, using their nose, they try to sniff it out. When they have no luck, they stand on a chair and try to sniff it out. Finally, they track the smell to the curtain behind the sofa. They look behind the curtain find some cheese, getting older, mouldier and smellier by the minute.

What You Need

- some cheese, fish or other smelly food

- an open container to put the food in

The Set-up

1. Buy some smelly cheese, a small bit of fish or some other type of smelly food. It should be fresh when you buy it, so that it does not smell straight away. You want the smell to develop slowly over a few days or even a couple of weeks. That will make it even more irritating for the victim.

59

2. Put the food in an open container and hide the container in a place where it cannot be easily seen. If the victim has a pet, do not leave it on the ground. Otherwise the pet will eat it and the joke will not work. Apart from behind a curtain, other good hiding places are underneath the sofa (taped to the bottom), on top of a cupboard, behind a row of books on the bookshelf, and behind a stereo system.

3. Don't let on that you can smell anything until the victim mentions it. Otherwise they may get suspicious and figure out that it was you who planted the food.

4. If you really want to make an impression, you could plant food in different places throughout the victim's house. But you'd better not let them know who did it. They might make you eat the rotten food when they've found it all.

Set-up Tip

- You don't have to plant the food in someone's house. The back of the car is a good place. So is your classroom.

We had fish and chips a week ago... it smells like a piece of it has crawled under this chair... and died!

Number 29:
Sugar and Salt

This is one of the oldest jokes around. It's an easy way to play havoc with someone's taste buds.

The Sting

The victim sits down to a nice hot cup of coffee. They've been working hard and looking forward to this drink all day. They grab the sugar container and pour sugar into their cup. They then stir the liquid and take a sip. Imagine their horror when their coffee tastes of salt instead of sugar.

What You Need

- a sugar container
- a salt container
- two saucers

The Set-up

1. Grab the salt and sugar containers at your victim's house.
2. Place the two saucers in front of you.
3. Pour the contents of the sugar container onto one saucer.
4. Pour the contents of the salt container onto the other saucer.
5. Pour the sugar from the saucer into the salt container.
6. Pour the salt from the saucer into the sugar container.
7. Put the containers back where you found them.
8. Try and be there when the victim gets a taste sensation they are not expecting.

9. This is a particularly good joke to play in a school cafeteria. Tell a few of your friends what you have done and have a laugh together as someone pours the wrong substance on their food or in their drink.

Number 30: Salt and Pepper

Like the Sugar and Salt practical joke, this joke tricks people into shaking the wrong seasoning onto their food.

The Sting

The victim sits down to dinner. They taste their meal and decide that they need a little bit of salt. They grab the salt container and start shaking. To their amazement, pepper starts coming out. They take another look at the container, but it definitely contains salt. They can see the salt through the glass. They shake again. Still, pepper comes out. They grab the pepper container and start shaking. Salt comes out. They finally got what they wanted, but they have no idea why there is salt coming out of the pepper container and pepper coming out of the salt container.

What You Need

- see-through salt and pepper containers
- a paper serviette or baking paper
- a pair of scissors

The Set-up

1. Make sure that the salt and pepper containers you are going to use are see-through. This means that the salt and pepper must be visible from the outside.

2. The containers must also have screw-top lids.

3. Unscrew the lids and turn the lids upside down on a table.

4. Pour some pepper into one of the upturned lids.

5. Pour some salt into the other upturned lid.

6. Cut out two pieces of the serviette or baking paper.

(A)

7. Place one of the pieces of paper on top of the salt in the upturned lid and press it so that the salt cannot fall out.

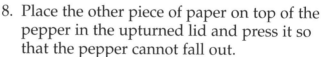

salt lid   Pepper lid

(B)

8. Place the other piece of paper on top of the pepper in the upturned lid and press it so that the pepper cannot fall out.

9. Screw the lid with salt onto the pepper container, then screw the lid with pepper onto the salt container. The victim will see salt in a container but, when they shake it, pepper will come out. The opposite will occur with the pepper container.

(C)

Number 31: What a Mess

This joke can be played with salt, pepper and sugar containers.

The Sting

The victim sits down to have breakfast. They pour some cereal into a bowl and add their milk. They then grab the sugar container and turn it upside down so that the sugar sprinkles onto their cereal. However, as soon as the sugar container is upside down, the lid falls off and the entire contents of the container pour on top of their cereal.

What You Need

• a salt, sugar or pepper container with a screw-top lid

The Set-up

1. Take the salt, pepper or sugar container and unscrew the lid until it is right off.

2. Place the lid on top of the container. It should look as if it is sitting on the container properly, but it is really not attached at all.

3. Put the container back in place. When someone goes to use it, the lid will come right off when they turn it upside down.

WOH! That's one scary sugar container! At least it's not my turn to use it next... It's DAD's!

Number 32:
The Bottomless Cup

This is another joke involving sugar and a sugar container. A laugh is guaranteed, as is a mess.

The Sting

The victim has just woken up and made their way to the kitchen. They are still a bit sleepy. They get the breakfast cereal out of the cupboard, the milk out of the fridge and a clean bowl and spoon from the dishwasher. They sit down at the breakfast table, pour the cereal into their bowl and add a splash of milk. They then decide to sprinkle a bit of sugar on top of the cereal. The sugar is in a plastic cup, not a container. They reach for the plastic cup and lift it towards them. The sugar pours all over the table, making a huge mess. The victim turns the cup upside down and sees that it has no bottom.

What You Need

- a plastic cup (not see-through)

- a pair of scissors

- sugar

The Set-up

1. Cut the bottom out of the plastic cup. Do not put a lid on the cup because you want the victim to see that it has sugar inside. However, you do not want a see-through cup, as they might notice it does not have a bottom.

2. Position the cup where the victim will find it. Once the sugar is in the cup, you will not be able to move it.

3. Pour the victim's sugar from their sugar container into the plastic cup.

4. Hide the victim's real sugar container. (Don't worry about the victim becoming suspicious that the sugar is in a different container. They will probably think that someone broke the other container or that it is dirty.)

5. Leave the room and wait for the cry when the victim picks the cup up.

6. Alternatively, you could make sure you are in the kitchen when you know the victim will use the sugar. That way you'll see the action first hand.

Similar Jokes

This practical joke is not restricted to sugar. You can cut the bottom out of any cheap plastic, cardboard or paper container. Here are a few suggestions:

- cereal packets

- bags of sugar

- bags of flour

- bags of rice

Don't cut the bottom out of a container full of liquid. The liquid will just spill out before you get to play the joke.

Just watch Mum's face in the morning when she picks up the breakfast cereal and it does...

THIS!

BREAKFAST SURPRISE

Number 33:
An Odd Vintage

Oh my! What was the chicken eating when it layed these eggs..?

GRAPES

Some wine drinkers are very fussy about the quality of the wine they drink. This joke is aimed at adults who think they know a lot about wine.

The Sting

Your victim is sitting down for dinner. You offer to get them a glass of wine. You fetch their wineglass and place it in front of them. You then fetch an egg-carton. Your victim is wondering what you're doing. They are in a state of shock when you pull an egg out, crack it on the edge of their glass and split it in two. An egg-full of wine pours into their glass.

What You Need

- an egg
- some wine
- a pin
- a bowl
- water
- glue
- a beaker

The Set-up

1. Using the pin, prick a tiny hole at each end of the eggshell.

2. Put one end of the eggshell to your mouth and blow as hard as you can. It will take some effort, but eventually you'll manage to blow all of the egg out.

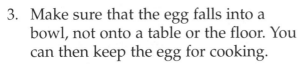

3. Make sure that the egg falls into a bowl, not onto a table or the floor. You can then keep the egg for cooking.

4. Run some water through the empty shell. This washes the insides out. Repeat this several times.

5. Glue up one of the holes.

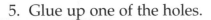

6. Carefully pour some wine into the remaining hole. This will take some time and a steady hand. You'll probably have to pour the wine into a beaker first.

7. When the eggshell is full, glue up the remaining hole. You are now ready to play the joke.

Similar Joke

- Rather than fill the eggshell up with wine, you could fill it up with water and return it to its carton. Imagine the shock someone will get next time they go to make an omelette or boil an egg.

Number 34: Wine Tasting

Here's another joke involving wine. You can play it when you're at a restaurant with your family. This practical joke doesn't really have a victim, but it will probably embarrass your parents and baffle the waiter.

The Sting

Your family is at a fancy restaurant for a special occasion. Everyone is dressed up and on their best behaviour. The waiter takes the food and wine orders and then returns to your table with the wine for the adults. The waiter shows the wine label to one of the adults, then opens the bottle and pours a little bit into the glass. The adult is now supposed to smell and taste the wine to make sure it is okay. However, before they do so, you reach over and put a thermometer into the wine and declare to the waiter that the wine is fine.

What You Need

- a thermometer
- a wineglass
- a bottle of wine

The Set-up

1. Before going to a fancy restaurant with your family or a group of adults, buy or borrow a thermometer.

2. Make sure that the thermometer is not too old and is in good condition. The best one to use is a thermometer probe with a plastic casing. It will not break and let dangerous substances such as mercury leak out.

3. Hide the thermometer somewhere in your clothing.

Do not put it in the back pocket of your pants in case you sit on it and break it.

4. When you see the waiter approaching with the wine, get the thermometer ready.

5. As soon as the waiter finishes pouring the sample wine, reach over and put the thermometer in the wineglass.

6. Give the wine a stir, then take the thermometer out and pretend to study the reading.

7. Turn to the waiter, put on a posh accent and say something like, 'The wine is perfect, thank you,' or 'It's probably a couple of degrees too warm but I'm sure we can cope with that'.

Number 35: Sliced Banana

This is a very clever joke that will leave the victim baffled.

The Sting

The victim grabs a banana from their fruit bowl. They snap open the peel at the top, then peel the sides. They can't believe what they see inside. The banana has been cut into slices, all the way down. It looks ready to go into a fruit salad. They have no idea how this happened, and if you don't tell them, they never will.

What You Need

Oh Mum's just a real joker.... She's always slipping genetically engineered bananas into my lunchbox!

What a sense of humour ...huh?

- a banana

- a needle

- a victim who likes eating bananas

The Set-up

1. Pick a banana with a firm skin.

2. Take the needle and poke it through the banana skin, near the top.

3. Wiggle the needle from side to side. This action slices the banana.

4. Take the needle out and poke it back in the banana skin a little further down.

5. Repeat the wiggling action.

6. Do the same in several places all the way down the banana.

7. When you have finished, put the banana at the top of the fruit bowl. Then wait for a victim to come along.

Follow-up

- If you are near the victim when they peel the banana, tell them that you heard on the radio about a new type of banana that slices itself as it grows. Explain that these bananas are grown especially to be used in fruit salads. If the victim believes  you, they may go and tell other people about this amazing new type of banana.

Number 36: Jelly Juice

This joke will really frustrate anyone who is very thirsty and wants a drink of juice. No matter how much they shake the bottle, the juice just won't come out.

The Sting

The victim is very thirsty. They go to the fridge and take out a bottle of juice. They get a glass from the cupboard and unscrew the lid from the bottle. They then tip the bottle and try to pour the juice into the glass. The only problem is that the juice won't come out. They can see the juice inside, but it just won't flow. They have a good look inside the bottle. There's nothing blocking the juice. They try once more, then give up and have a glass of water instead.

What You Need

- a bottle of juice
- an empty container
- some jelly

The Set-up

1. Take a bottle of juice.

2. Pour the juice into an empty container and keep it to drink later.

3. Following the instructions on the jelly packet, make the jelly mixture in the juice bottle. (Make sure that the colour of the jelly is the same as the colour of the juice.)

4. Hide the bottle in the back of the fridge to set.

5. When the jelly has set, put the bottle where the juice usually is.

6. Wait for the victim to grab the bottle, then walk past and enjoy the look of frustration on their face.

Similar Jokes

- Rather than replace the juice with jelly, you could put the bottle in the freezer and return it to the fridge when the juice has frozen. The victim won't be able to get a drink of juice this way either.

- Another suggestion is to empty the juice out of the bottle, then pour some paint, the same colour as the juice, into the bottle. Swirl the paint around until it covers the bottle, pour out any excess paint, then let it set. When the paint is completely dry, pour some water into the bottle. The victim will get the shock of their life when water comes out, instead of juice. (Make sure the victim does not drink any of the paint, though!)

Number 37: A Little Extra

One of the best things about A Little Extra is that there can be a number of victims.

The Sting

The whole family is sitting down for their evening meal. It's their favourite, spaghetti bolognaise. The bowl of spaghetti is handed around and everyone serves themselves. Then the bolognaise sauce is handed around and everyone scoops some out and pours it on top of their spaghetti. It smells so good. After the cheese is added, they tuck into their meal. The first person to swallow a mouthful screams and runs to the water tap. Suddenly, a second person follows. Then a third and a fourth. The bolognaise sauce has been tampered with and is so spicy that no one can eat it.

What You Need

- a hot, spicy food additive
- a water supply where the meal is served

The Set-up

1. Get hold of a hot, spicy food additive. There may be some in your kitchen cupboard. Otherwise, you'll have to buy the additive from the store. Below are a few examples of the type of additive you can use:

- curry powder
- paprika
- chilli powder

- pepper
- tabasco sauce

2. Take out the additive when someone is cooking a spaghetti sauce or a stew or casserole. These are ideal meals to add an additive to because the additive will usually blend in and not be noticed until it is tasted.

3. When the cook leaves the kitchen, sneak in and pour your additive into the food. Stir it very well, then leave the cooking implements exactly as they were when the cook left the kitchen.

4. When the dinner is served and the victims start reaching for water, do the same. That way you won't be suspected of having played the joke.

Set-up Tips

- Never play this joke if one of the possible victims is allergic to the food additive you are going to add. You do not want to make someone sick.

This much CHILLI POWDER in the spaghetti sauce will guarantee takeaway burgers for dinner tonight.

- The best day to play this joke is when you feel like takeaway food. When the joke takes effect, it will be too late to cook another meal, so the whole family will have to get takeaway.

- Many cooks taste their creations as they are cooking. If this is the case with your cook, then you are going to have to add the hot, spicy additive just before the meal is served.

Number 38:
Movie Munchies

This joke may seem a little bit revolting, but you actually don't do anything revolting at all. It's all about planting an idea in the victim's mind.

The Sting

The victim, a friend of yours, is sitting at the movies. The advertisements and trailers have just finished and the main feature is about to start. The lights go out. You offer the victim a box of Maltesers, saying you are too full to finish them. The victim accepts and eats one of them. You then say something that makes the victim think twice about eating the rest of the Maltesers. It also spoils their enjoyment of the film. What is it that you say? Read the Set-up to find out.

What You Need

- a movie theatre

- a box of Maltesers, Jaffas, Kool Mints or other round, smooth sweets

The Set-up

1. Make sure you are sitting next to the victim in the movie theatre.

2. When the lights are completely out, hand over an opened box of Maltesers, Jaffas, Kool Mints or other round, smooth sweets.

3. Tell the victim that you are too full to eat them.

4. Wait until the victim has eaten one or two of the sweets and then say to the victim, 'By the way, I put one of the sweets up my nose and then put it back in the box'.

5. You haven't really put a sweet up your nose but the victim doesn't know this. They have to decide whether to believe you or not.

6. As the victim has already eaten a couple of the sweets, they will probably feel sick thinking that one of them could have been up your nose.

7. If they decide to eat the rest of the box, they will feel very uneasy throughout the movie. It is amazing how slimy these sweets feel when you have been told that one of them has been up someone's nose.

Good movie hey? How are you enjoying my sweets? Have you found the one I had up my nose?

Number 39: Balancing an Egg

The only difficult part of this joke is getting the victim to agree to take part. Once they've agreed, the rest is easy.

The Sting

The victim is standing on one side of an open door. They place their fingers through the gap between the door and the doorframe, so that their fingers appear on the other side of the door. An egg is placed on top of those fingers. Then the victim finds themselves alone. How do they get out of this mess without dropping the egg? They can't.

What You Need

- a room with a large gap between the door and the doorframe

- an egg

The Set-up

1. Find a victim who has a room with a large gap between the door and the doorframe. That way, any mess the victim makes will be on their floor.

2. Tell the victim that you were recently taught a really cool game.

3. Open the door and get the victim to put two fingers through the gap. Assure them that you will not slam the door on their fingers.

4. Take an egg and place it on their fingers.

5. Smile and walk away. The victim cannot move away from the door without dropping the egg.

MUCH LATER....

Similar Jokes

- There are other objects that you can use for this joke, other than an egg. Try a small cup of water or a small cup of flour.

- If you use a cup of fizzy drink, drop an M&M into the drink. This will cause it to fizz all over the victim's hand.

Word Jokes

Some practical jokes are word games. They involve tricking or confusing people with words or phrases. After the joke, the victim will feel very foolish because they will realise how easily they were tricked.

Number 40: Four and Out

This joke almost always works. It is quick and easy and makes the victim kick themselves for being made a fool of so easily.

The Sting

You tell the victim that they won't be able to give incorrect answers to four questions. Of course, the victim claims that they can easily give four incorrect answers. How easy it seems to them. They give an incorrect answer to the first question. Then they give an incorrect answer to the second question. Then they give an incorrect answer to the third question. One question to go and they are feeling very confident indeed. You throw in a comment that requires them to answer. They give a correct answer without realising that this is the fourth question.

them to answer. They give a correct answer without realising that this is the fourth question.

What You Need

- nothing, except a victim

The Set-up

1. Tell your victim that you bet they can't give an incorrect answer to four questions you're going to ask them. They'll probably be so confident that you can bet them some money or get them to be your servant for a day if they fail the task.

Do I look like your dear old Granny?

It's a trick question, so I'll have to say Yes... Even though my Grandma would not be happy to hear me say that!

2. Make the first question an easy one. Something like 'Are you a boy?'. To give the incorrect answer, boys would answer 'No' and girls would answer 'Yes'. If they give the correct answer, then you've won your bet already.

3. Make the second question another easy one or even a silly one. Something like 'Am I your grandparent?'. They should answer 'Yes', as this is the incorrect answer. If they answer 'No', you've won.

4. The third question can also be easy. Ask them what day of the week it is. If they answer with today's day, you've won. If they answer with the wrong day, they're still in the contest. They're probably also feeling very confident.

5. Now, instead of asking the fourth question like the previous ones, say 'That's three questions I've asked now, isn't it?'. They will not expect that this is the fourth question and will answer 'Yes'. You then tell them that they have answered the fourth question correctly and have therefore lost the bet.

Number 41: The Paper Tube

This word joke does not only rely on the words you use. It also relies on what you show the victim.

The Sting

The victim is shown a piece of paper with a tiny hole in the middle of it. They are then asked whether they can push a finger through the centre of the paper without tearing the paper. Of course, they will say it is impossible. When you claim that you can do it, they'll either have a go and fail or they'll say that you can't do it. Then it's your turn to show them exactly how it's done. The trick is in the words that you use. The small hole is just put in the paper to mislead the victim.

What You Need

- paper (preferably more than one piece)
- a pin or pair of scissors

How do I stick my finger through that tiny hole in the paper? I'd have about as much chance trying to poke a fully loaded school bus through there!

The Set-up

1. Using a pin or a pair of scissors, make a small hole in the middle of a piece of paper. The hole must be big enough to see but small enough not to allow a finger to pass through it.

2. Make a similar hole in another piece of paper. You may need this piece if the victim decides to take up your challenge and tears the other piece.

3. Hold one piece of paper up, showing your victim the hole. Then ask your victim the following question,

making sure you use these exact words: 'Do you think you can push your finger through the centre of the paper without tearing it?'.

4. When your victim says it can't be done, or after they've had an attempt and failed, tell them that you can do it.

5. Take the piece of paper and roll it into a tube. Then put your finger into the tube. You are pushing your finger through the centre of the paper without tearing it, just as you said you could.

Number 42: My Left Elbow

For this joke to work, you must say the crucial words exactly as they are written in the Set-up section.

The Sting

You tell the victim that you can write with your left elbow. Of course they won't believe you. You insist that it is possible and that they should have a try. They may try to balance the pen on their elbow and then write, but they'll probably just tell you that it's impossible. You tell them that you'll show them how it's done if they'll polish your shoes for a month. When they agree, you do exactly as you said you would. You write with your left elbow.

What You Need

- a piece of paper

- a pen

The Set-up

1. Put a pen and a piece of paper in front of your victim.

2. Say the following words exactly: 'I can write with my left elbow'. After you have said those words, you might like to add something like, 'I bet you can't do it' or 'Will you buy me an ice cream if I can do it?'.

3. When your victim says it can't be done, or after they've had an attempt and failed, tell them you'll show them how.

4. Roll up your sleeve and try to balance the pen on your left elbow. You can even get a cloth out and rub your elbow in preparation. It doesn't matter what you do to your elbow because you're not actually going to use it. It is just part of the act.

5. Grab the pen in your hand and write the following words on the piece of paper: 'with my left elbow'.

6. Show the piece of paper to your friend and say, 'See, I told you that I could write "with my left elbow"'.

Computer Jokes

There are many practical jokes that can be done to someone's computer. All you need is a bit of time alone at the victim's computer. There are many computer jokes that can be downloaded from Internet sites. These often cost money. The jokes in this chapter do not require downloads and are free. The instructions in this chapter are for people using Microsoft® Windows®.

Number 43:
The Fast Mouse

Speedy Gonzales and Stuart Little have nothing on this mouse. This one moves so quickly, your victim won't even have time to blink.

The Sting

The victim of this joke sits down at their computer to surf the Net or do some homework. They go to use their mouse. The cursor starts whizzing around the screen at twice the normal speed or is so slow the victim gets very frustrated.

What You Need

- the victim's computer
- two minutes alone with the computer

The Set-up

1. Make sure the victim is distracted for a couple of minutes. Perhaps arrange for one of your friends to ring the victim at a particular time, when both you and your victim are at the victim's house.

2. Click the Start button on the computer taskbar.

3. Move the cursor to the Settings tag.

4. Click on Control Panel. The Control Panel box should open up.

5. Click on the icon for the Mouse. (If there is no Mouse icon, then click on 'view all Control Panel options', then click on the Mouse icon.) The Mouse Properties box should open up.

6. There should be a tag that reads Motion or Pointer Options. Press on this tag. It allows you to alter the speed of the mouse. Make the changes that you want, then press Apply.

7. Close all the boxes so that the computer looks exactly the way it did before you touched it.

Similar Jokes

- There are other alterations you can make to the mouse. You can change the size and shape of the pointer, as well as the designs that appear when certain mouse functions take place. You can also change the functions of the buttons on the mouse and the clicking speed of the buttons.

Number 44: New Screensaver

Here's an opportunity to make your mark on someone else's computer, without doing any lasting damage. If your victim's confused enough, they may even think their entire computer has been replaced.

The Sting

The victim of this joke leaves their computer for a few minutes to get something to eat, answer the phone, or for another reason. When they return, their normal screensaver has disappeared and been replaced by one that has a message saying 'You have been stung by [Your Name]' or 'I have gobbled up your screensaver', or by a humorous image.

What You Need

- the victim's computer
- three minutes alone with the computer

The Set-up

1. Make sure the victim is distracted for at least three minutes. Perhaps arrange for one of your friends to ring the victim at a particular time, when both you and your victim are at the victim's house.

2. Click the Start button on the computer taskbar.

3. Move the cursor to the Settings tag.

4. Click on Control Panel. The Control Panel box should open up.

5. Click on the icon that reads Display. The Display Properties box should open up.

6. There should be a tag that reads Screen Saver. Press on this tag. It allows you to change the screensaver.

7. There is a box that contains a list of all the possible screensavers. Press on the arrow to the left of this box to bring up the choices. Select one, then press Apply.

8. If you choose Scrolling Marquee, then Settings, a box comes up allowing you to type in a message. This message will scroll across the screen when the screensaver is activated.

9. Close all the boxes so that the computer looks exactly the way it did before you touched it.

Similar Joke

You can also change the amount of time it takes for the screensaver to appear. Why not change the time to one minute, so that if the computer is idle for this short period, the screensaver will pop up. The victim will start getting very annoyed indeed.

Number 45: New Wallpaper

Changing wallpaper usually involves hours of stripping, plastering and gluing. With this trick, you can change the wallpaper in minutes, with no mess at all.

The Sting

The victim of this joke leaves their computer for a few minutes to get something to eat, answer the phone, or for another reason. When they return, their normal background, also known as wallpaper, has disappeared and been replaced by one with a humorous image.

What You Need

- the victim's computer
- three minutes alone with the computer

The Set-up

1. Make sure the victim is distracted for at least three minutes. Perhaps arrange for one of your friends to ring the victim at a particular time, when both you and your victim are at the victim's house.

2. Click the Start button on the computer taskbar.

3. Move the cursor to the Settings tag.

4. Click on Control Panel. The Control Panel box should open up.

5. Click on the icon that reads Display. The Display Properties box should open up.

6. There should be a tag that reads Background. Press on this tag. It allows you to change the computer's background image.

7. There is a box that contains a list of all the possible background images. Select one, then press Apply.

8. Close all the boxes so that the computer looks exactly the way it did before you touched it.

Similar Joke

• You can also change the way an image appears on the screen by clicking on Center, Tile or Stretch in the Background box.

Number 46: Dancing Keys

Turn the best speller in the world into someone who can't even spell their name correctly. Not even the spell check can help them with this joke.

The Sting

The victim of this joke leaves their computer for a few minutes to get something to eat, answer the phone, or for another reason. When they return, everything appears normal, until they begin to type. To their amazement, the keys on their keyboard seem to have moved around.

What You Need

- the victim's computer

- a small screwdriver

- two minutes alone with the computer

The Set-up

1. Make sure the victim is distracted for at least two minutes. Perhaps arrange for one of your friends to ring the victim at a particular time, when both you and your victim are at the victim's house.

2. Put the sharp end of a screwdriver under one of the keyboard keys and lift it off. Be careful not to do any damage.

3. Repeat the process with a number of other keys.

4. Clip each key into the wrong place on the keyboard.

5. Make sure that all the keys are in place when the victim returns to the computer.

Set-up Tips

- Try changing as many keys as you can—this will cause maximum chaos and frustration.

- Another thing to do is just swap two keys around. This will confuse the victim even more than changing all of the keys because they may not know why the error is occurring.

Telephone Jokes

Some of the jokes in this chapter involve changing commands on a telephone. Others involve making funny telephone calls. It used to be very easy to get away with making funny telephone calls to people. However, these days you need to take a few precautions. Make sure that the number you are calling from cannot be traced. Either make the call from a public phone or block the receiver's ability to trace you.

Number 47: The Dusty Phone

This joke is really only appropriate if the victim has a cord phone, with the receiver connected to the handset.

The Sting

The victim gets a phone call from a representative of the telephone company. The victim is told that in ten minutes time, the telephone lines are going to be cleared of dust. To prepare for this, the victim is told to leave the phone off the hook and put a bag over the receiver so that it collects any dust that blows out of the holes and doesn't wreck the victim's carpet.

What You Need

- the telephone number of your victim

- someone who can pose as the representative of the telephone company, without laughing and without being recognised by the victim

The Set-up

1. Find out when the victim will be home alone. You want them to answer the phone.

2. Ring up (or get someone else to ring up) and introduce yourself as a representative of the telephone company.

3. Tell the victim that the company is currently cleaning the telephone lines in their area. This is done by blasting air through the lines to clear any dust. In ten minutes time, it will be the turn of the victim's line.

4. Instruct the victim to leave the phone off the hook and to put a bag over the receiver. This will stop dust ruining the victim's carpet.

5. Thank the victim, then hang up.

6. Laugh as you imagine your victim standing next to the phone, waiting for air to be blasted through the line.

Set-up Tips

- It is very important that the person posing as the telephone company representative sound as convincing as possible. They'll need to have answers ready for any questions that the victim might ask, such as 'How long will I need to keep the bag over the phone?' and 'What sort of equipment do you use to clear the lines?'.

- Make sure the person posing as the telephone company representative knows the name of the victim and refers to them by that name. Otherwise the victim may guess that it is a joke. After all, the telephone company would have their name.

Follow-up

- If you believe that the victim is going to follow your instructions, ring them back about ten minutes later and tell them that the telephone company engineers discovered a new form of dust that is invisible to the human eye. Tell them to dispose of the bag carefully, being sure not to let any of the dust escape because it could cause a massive carpet stain in forty-eight hours time.

Number 48:
Collecting Your Messages

This joke can be played on someone answering the phone or to an answering machine.

The Sting

The victim gets a phone call from someone asking for Joe Bloggs (or any other name). The victim explains that the caller must have the wrong number because Joe Bloggs does not live there. Not long after, another caller rings and asks for Joe Bloggs. This continues a number of times. The victim is getting more and more heated up. Finally, someone rings up and says, 'Hi, it's Joe Bloggs here. Have you got any messages for me?'.

What You Need

- the telephone number of your victim

- a number of people who can pose as callers without being recognised by the victim

The Set-up

1. Ring up the victim and ask to speak to Joe Bloggs (or any name other than the victim's).

2. An hour later, get a second person to ring up and ask to speak to Joe Bloggs.

3. An hour later, get a third person to ring up and ask to speak to Joe Bloggs.

4. An hour later, get a fourth person to ring up and ask to speak to Joe Bloggs.

5. When you have had as many different people as possible ring up, make another call. This time, say, 'Hi, it's Joe Bloggs here. Have you got any messages for me?'.

Set-up Tips

- This joke can be over in a couple of hours or it can drag on for weeks. You can have your callers ring the victim one after the other, before you ring up claiming to be Joe Bloggs. Or you can arrange it so that the victim receives a call every day or two for a few weeks, before you ring up claiming to be Joe Bloggs.

- Try to get your callers to each say something different, rather than all ringing up and asking 'Is Joe Bloggs there?'. For example, one could be a telemarketer trying to sell something to Joe Bloggs. Another could be Joe's mother trying to get hold of him. Yet another could be a debt collector chasing Joe because he owes them money. The more variety, the better the joke.

- Of course, if the victim turns out to have the same name as the person you are leaving messages for, then you're going to have to do some pretty quick thinking.

Follow-up

- If you know the victim's address as well as their phone number, you could send a few letters to Joe Bloggs, after you have finished with the telephone joke. Then ring the victim up a few days later and claim to be Joe Bloggs again. Ask the victim if they have any mail for you.

Number 49:
The Electrocution

This joke is played on the victim when they answer their phone. It does not work nearly as well if messages are left on an answering machine. It can be played on a victim with a cord phone, a cordless phone or a mobile phone.

The Sting

The victim gets a phone call from a representative of the telephone company. The victim is told that there is some trouble with their telephone line and that the telephone company is currently trying to fix it. The victim is told not to answer their telephone in the next few minutes, otherwise the caller may receive an electric shock. A few minutes later, the victim receives another phone call. When they pick up the phone, the caller screams 'Owwwwwww'.

What You Need

- the telephone number of your victim

- someone who can pose as the representative of the telephone company, without laughing and without being recognised by the victim

- someone who can pose as the second caller and do a convincing impersonation of someone being electrocuted

The Set-up

1. Find out when the victim will be home alone. You want them to answer the phone.

2. Ring up (or get someone else to ring up) and introduce yourself as a representative of the telephone company.

3. Tell the victim that the company has identified a problem with their line and that it is about to be fixed.

4. Instruct the victim to hang up and not pick up the phone for at least ten minutes, otherwise the caller may receive an electric shock.

5. Give a little giggle at the end, so that the caller is unsure whether it is a joke or not.

6. About ten minutes later, get someone to ring the victim. When the victim picks up the receiver, the caller should yell as if receiving an electric shock.

Set-up Tips

- Although the caller pretending to be the telephone company representative has to be as convincing as possible, this joke relies on the victim not quite believing the telephone company representative. In most cases, when the victim gets the second call, the victim will hesitate, then pick up the phone out of curiosity.

- Make sure the person pretending to be the telephone company representative knows the name of the victim and refers to them by that name. Otherwise the victim may guess that it is all a joke. After all, the telephone company would have their name.

Mum... you remember when I was talking to that person from the phone company... and they got an electric shock... well.... apparently we shut down the whole power grid!

I wonder what happened to that poor lady on the phone?

- You do not want to leave your victim with the impression that they have caused someone to be electrocuted. Before the second caller hangs up, they should let the victim know it was a joke.

102

Follow-up

- You can extend the joke by sending the victim a fake electricity bill for 'Extra electricity used by telephone at 6.30 p.m. on Tuesday 6 April' (or whatever the time and date of the joke was).

Number 50: Emergency Call

This joke involves leaving a message on an answering machine. It does not work if someone answers the phone. Before ringing, make sure that your victim is out and that they have an answering machine. You can play this joke on a friend without disguising who you are.

The Sting

The victim gets home and sees they have a message on their answering machine. They press the 'Play' button and hear a message that says, 'Paula, [insert the victim's name instead] are you there? It's

Jill [insert your name instead]. Please answer the phone if you're home. I need your help urgently. I think there's someone in my house and they're about to ...' The message then cuts off.

What You Need

- the telephone number of your victim

- a victim with an answering machine

The Set-up

1. Make sure there is no one at the victim's house.

2. Ring up the victim.

3. Once the answering machine kicks in, put on a panicky voice, as if you are in trouble. Leave a message like, 'Paula, [insert the victim's name instead] are you there?

It's Jill [insert your name instead]. Please answer the phone if you're home. I need your help urgently. I think there's someone in my house and they're about to ...'

4. Finally, gasp for breath and hang-up in mid-sentence.

Set-up Tips

- You do not want your victim to panic and call the police after hearing your call. To avoid this, leave them another message immediately after the first. In this message, just say 'Paula, it's Jill. Only joking'.

- If you know when your victim is likely to get home, you could hide near their house and sneak to their front door when they go inside. Then listen for the phone message. As soon as it finishes, knock on the door. When they answer, say 'Surprise', or dress yourself up in torn clothes and fake blood.

Similar Joke

- Rather than scare the victim, you can frustrate them by ringing up and leaving a message saying, 'Hi Paula, it's Jill. You won't believe this. I just got offered two free tickets to [the name of a concert or sports event that you know the victim would love to attend]. The problem is they have to be picked up within the next half an hour and I can't get away from what I'm doing. If you want one of the tickets, ring me up by 5 p.m. and I'll tell you where to pick them up from. It's just around the corner from your place. If you're later than 5, don't bother calling. The tickets will have gone'. Of course, you have to know that your friend will be away for at least half an hour.

PICK UP THE FREE TICKETS FOR THE GRAND FINAL by 5·00PM!! I've got 13 seconds to run three blocks!

I'll do anything for a free ticket!

Number 51:
The Contest Winner

Like Emergency Call, this joke involves leaving a message on an answering machine. It does not work if someone answers the phone.

The Sting

The victim gets home and sees they have a message on their answering machine. They press the 'Play' button and hear a message that says, 'This is a message for Pete [insert victim's name instead]. We are calling because you have won a great prize. It includes a holiday, spending money, a brand new mountain bike and a big-screen TV. To claim your prize, all you have to do is ring 9863 5 "beep beep beep"'. The victim jumps up and down because it appears as if the answering machine has cut out before the person has given the full telephone number.

What You Need

- the telephone number of your victim
- a victim with an answering machine
- a tape recorder

The Set-up

1. Make sure there is no one at the victim's house.
2. Ring up the victim.
3. When the answering machine kicks in, leave a message

pretending you are calling from a radio station to tell the victim they have won a fantastic prize. All the victim has to do is call a particular phone number by the end of the day.

4. Start giving out a phone number. When you have got three numbers left, hang up suddenly.

Set-up Tips

- When making the call, disguise your voice or get someone the victim doesn't know to leave the message.

- Write down exactly what you are going to say, then read it out. This will make it sound more professional and less like you are making things up as you go along.

- The 'beep beep beep' sound that appears at the end is not really coming from their answering machine but is a sound you make. You could say it yourself and make it sound like a machine, or you could tape the sound of your own answering machine beeping, then play the sound back.

Follow-up

- You can extend the joke the next day by leaving a message that says, 'Hi Pete. We called yesterday about the great prize you've won. We'll give you another day to call us, then offer the prize to someone else. In case you've lost our phone number, it is 9863 5 "beep beep beep"'.

OH MY PRIZE...!
MY PRIZE...!

BEEP BEEP BEEP

Number 52: Wrong Numbers

This joke results in the victim ringing lots of wrong numbers. It's great fun listening to the confusion that you have caused. This will only work on phones with automatic dial buttons.

The Sting

Your victim wants to phone someone they talk with regularly. They talk to this person so often that they have them on automatic dial. That means the victim has programmed their phone to automatically dial a particular number when a particular button is pressed. The victim presses the button that they always press. But they get through to someone else. They try again but the same thing happens. When they try another automatic dial number, they get another wrong number. They soon discover that all of their automatic dial numbers have been changed.

What You Need

- a victim with a telephone with automatic dial buttons

- about ten minutes to carry out the joke

The Set-up

1. Make sure the victim's phone has automatic dial buttons that they have programmed. The best indication that someone uses the automatic dial function on their phone is a sticker with someone's name under or next to each button.

2. You then have to work out how to change the numbers. See if you can find the instruction booklet for the phone. It will contain the instructions that you need.

3. You can put in completely new numbers at random or the phone numbers of people you know.

4. If you know the phone numbers for all the people listed on the automatic dial buttons, you could swap these phone numbers around. That will really confuse the victim.

5. If you don't know how to change the numbers, just swap the stickers around. This will confuse the victim for a short time.

Set-up Tips

- Never change the number for an emergency service, such as a doctor or the local police station. People only phone these numbers in emergencies and you don't want your joke to cause distress.

- Don't replace one of the automatic dial numbers with that of an emergency service. Emergency services are busy enough without having to deal with wrong numbers.

Number 53: Endless Ringing

This joke will only work with cord phones. It does not work with cordless or mobile phones.

The Sting

Your victim's phone rings. They pick up the receiver and say 'Hello'. The problem is that the phone keeps ringing. The victim slams the phone down and then picks it up again. It's still ringing. No matter what they do, the ringing won't stop until the person on the other end decides that your victim obviously isn't home. Your victim slams their receiver down. The next time the phone rings, the same thing happens.

What You Need

- a victim with a cord telephone

- some tape

- about ten minutes to carry out the joke

The Set-up

1. Pick up the receiver on the victim's phone.

2. Tape down the clip that sits under the receiver. Normally, when the receiver is picked up, the clip lifts, allowing the person answering the phone to speak to the caller. If the clip is taped down, the phone just keeps ringing and the person answering the phone cannot speak to the caller. (Do not use dark or brightly coloured tape, otherwise the victim may see the tape when they lift the receiver up. Transparent tape is the best to use.)

3. Standby to listen to your victim get very, very frustrated.

4. This joke does not only work when the phone rings. If the victim picks up their receiver to make a call, they will not get a dial tone and will be unable to make a call.

Follow-up

- If you want to frustrate the caller even more than usual, you could be hiding nearby with a tape recorder. On your tape is a recording of their phone ringing. As soon as the real ringing stops, press the 'Play' button on your recorder. When they hear the ringing coming from somewhere else, they'll really think they're going mad.

Number 54: The Phantom Telephone

This joke doesn't involve an actual phone. However, it does involve the sound of a telephone ringing. It's designed to drive someone mad. The Phantom Telephone joke works best if the victim does not have a cordless phone.

The Sting

Your victim decides that they should do some gardening. They put on their gardening clothes and boots and go into the garden. They've been outside for a couple of minutes when they hear the telephone ringing. They take off their boots and go inside. As soon as they get in the door, the phone stops ringing. They go outside again and put their boots back on. After five minutes of gardening, they hear the telephone ringing again. They run for the door, take off their muddy boots and step inside. As soon as they do, the phone stops ringing again. This happens three or four times and your victim gets angrier and angrier each time.

What You Need

- a tape recorder
- the victim's telephone

The Set-up

It's always the way. The phone doesn't ring all day... Then as soon as you get knee deep in mud... SOMEBODY ALWAYS RINGS FOR THE FOURTH TIME!

RING RING RING RING

1. At least a day before you are going to play the joke, set your tape recorder up next to the victim's telephone.

2. Make sure that your victim is not in the house. If they see what you are doing, they will get suspicious.

3. Using a mobile phone, ring the number of the main phone. If you do not have a mobile phone, arrange for one of your friends to ring the number at a particular time.

4. While the phone is ringing, press the 'Record' button on your tape recorder and tape the ringing.

5. On the day of the joke, set the tape recorder up near the telephone. It has to appear as if the sound is coming from the phone. However, make sure that you and the tape recorder are hidden from view in case the victim makes it into the room.

6. Turn the volume of the tape recorder right up so that the victim will hear the ringing.

7. Wait until your victim is outside or is busy somewhere in the house. Then press the 'Play' button on your tape recorder.

8. As soon as the victim gets near the phone, turn the tape recorder off.

9. Rewind the tape and get ready to play the joke again.

10. Your victim doesn't have to be gardening for this joke to work. You can wait until they are doing almost any activity. Here are a few suggestions:

- when the victim is washing the car

- when the victim is outside practising their golf swing

- when the victim is having a bath

- when the victim is doing homework

Number 55: The Ear Ring

The result of this joke is that everyone except the victim will know that the victim has been stung.

The Sting

The victim's phone rings. They answer and have a long conversation. They have no idea that a practical joke is being played on them. Even when they put the telephone receiver down, they do not know that a practical joke has been played on them. They walk down the street to the shops. A few people stop and stare and giggle. The victim just ignores them and keeps walking. The shopkeepers laugh as they serve the victim, but the victim takes no notice. On the walk home, other people point and laugh. By now, the victim is wondering what everyone is laughing at. As soon as the victim gets home, they look in the mirror. One of their ears has a black ring around it.

What You Need

- the victim's telephone
- powder or paint

The Set-up

1. Get some water-based paint or some coloured powder that will stick to skin. Make-up powder is very good for this purpose. It does not have to be black paint or

powder. Consider a really wild, bright colour, like purple or orange.

2. Put the paint or powder around the inside rim of the victim's telephone receiver.

3. Put the telephone receiver back.

4. Wait for the victim to have a telephone conversation, then have a look at the ear that they held against the telephone. It should have a bright ring around it.

Parent Jokes

Although many of the jokes in this book can be played on your parents, there are some that are especially suited for this purpose. This chapter includes jokes you can use when you want to fool your folks.

Number 56: The Thread

This practical joke works best on mothers. Mothers just cannot resist tidying up their children and making sure that the clothes they are wearing are neat.

The Sting

You walk past your mother (or another family member). As you pass them, they notice that your shirt, jumper or jacket has a loose thread. Thinking they are doing you a favour, they grab the end of the loose thread and pull. They get a great shock when the thread gets longer and longer the more they pull it. They're going to have to pull the thread for a very long time to get to the end of it.

What You Need

- a spool of cotton

- a needle

- a parent or relative who cares enough about your appearance to be the victim of your joke

The Set-up

1. To make this joke convincing, the cotton should be the same colour as the shirt, jacket or jumper you are wearing. That way it will appear to be a loose thread that simply needs a firm tug to break it off.

2. Hide the spool of cotton up your sleeve, down your pants or somewhere else where it can't be seen.

3. Make sure that the cotton can flow off the spool easily.

4. Unroll some of the cotton and poke the end of it through an opening in your clothing, such as a collar or cuff. You may want to use a needle to thread the cotton through to the front of your clothing.

5. Let a fair bit of thread hang free, so that your victim cannot fail to notice it.

6. Get close to the victim and start a conversation. If they do not notice the thread, flick at it.

7. As they pull the thread, let it roll off the spool.

8. Act surprised, as if you have no idea what's happening.

Number 57: Strange Perfume

This joke is one to play on your mother, or even your big sister, just before they start getting ready for a special night out. If they don't notice that something's wrong, anyone who gets close enough to them certainly will.

The Sting

Your victim is getting ready for a special night out. They've had a bath or shower, they've dressed in a brand new outfit and they've put their make-up on. There's just one thing left. They have to put some of their new perfume on. They twist the lid off the perfume bottle and dab a little of the perfume on. Then they go out. So far they haven't realised that anything is wrong. It's only when someone comments that they smell of vinegar that they realise they've been the target of a practical joke.

What You Need

- a bottle of the victim's perfume

- some vinegar

- a clean, empty perfume container

The Set-up

1. Make sure that your mother (or big sister) is not around.

2. Unscrew the lid of their perfume bottle and pour the perfume into the clean container.

3. Fill the real perfume bottle with vinegar.

4. Screw the lid back on and put the perfume bottle back where it is normally kept.

5. Put the container with the real perfume somewhere safe. When the joke is over, the victim will want their real perfume back. Perfume is very expensive and they are not going to be very happy if you have thrown it away.

6. Wait for the victim to put their perfume on and see if they notice the switch.

Set-up Tips

- If the victim notices that their perfume has been switched, give them the real perfume back so that they can finish getting ready and go out.

- If the victim does not notice that their perfume has been switched, you may want to tell them before they leave the house. Otherwise, you may ruin their night.

- If you let the victim go out wearing the vinegar perfume, go back into their room and switch the liquids around again. To do this, pour the vinegar down the sink, rinse the perfume bottle, then pour the real perfume back in. The victim will never know why they smelt of vinegar instead of perfume.

Number 58: Strange Aftershave

This joke is similar to Strange Perfume, except that the victim is your father or older brother. The other difference is that this joke is discovered straight away. In fact, the victim gets quite a shock.

The Sting

Your victim is getting ready to have a shave. They have the shaving cream, shaving brush and razor blade in front of them. They lather their face with shaving cream, then carefully shave the whiskers on their face. Feeling good, they splash some water on their face, then dry their face with a towel. Finally, they reach for their bottle of aftershave, splash some into their hands and dab it onto their face. Then they scream. They scream loudly because their face is stinging. Somehow, their aftershave has turned into vinegar.

Now that I've finished my shave... I'll try on some of my new Father's Day

AAAHRFFTER SHAVE

What You Need

- a bottle of the victim's aftershave
- some vinegar
- a clean, empty container

The Set-up

1. Make sure that your father (or big brother) is not around.

2. Unscrew the lid of their aftershave bottle and pour the aftershave into the clean container.

3. Fill the aftershave bottle with vinegar. It has to be vinegar because other clear substances may not give the stinging effect that you are after.

4. Wait until you hear a screaming noise, then leave the house. You don't want to be around until your father or brother has had time to calm down.

5. Sneak back into the bathroom and replace the vinegar with the aftershave. To do this, pour the vinegar down the sink, rinse the aftershave bottle, then pour the real aftershave back in.

Special Note

Don't worry too much about the screaming from your victim. The vinegar causes a quick stinging sensation on skin that has been shaved. It causes no damage and your victim should see the funny side of the joke once they've had time to get over the shock.

Number 59: A New Outfit

The time to play this joke is when you've spotted a great shirt, pair of pants or skirt in a shop. You can't afford to buy it yourself and you doubt your parents will buy it for you. But if this joke is successful, the chances are you're going to have that new piece of clothing the same day.

The Sting

Your mother or father starts pulling wet clothes out of the washing machine. Suddenly they stop in shock. They pull out an item of your clothing that is ripped to shreds. It must have got caught up in one of the washing machine parts. When they show it to you, you get very upset. You may even burst into tears. You tell them it was your favourite item of clothing and that nothing could replace it. Then you suddenly remember that there is one item of clothing that could possibly replace it.

What You Need

- an old item of clothing

- a pair of scissors

- a washing machine

Mum! Mum! My favourite T-shirt! My shirt I can't live without! the best one in my entire wardrobe...

What did you do? Did you let Dad mow it before you washed it?

I can't make it through another day without a nice new one of these!

The Set-up

1. A few days before you play this joke, wear an old item of clothing and mention to your parents how much you like it. In reality, you should choose something you are not very keen on at all.

2. Wear the item of clothing at least once more over the next day or so.

3. When you're ready to play the joke, grab a pair of

scissors and make a few small cuts in the piece of clothing.

4. Make the cuts larger by ripping them with your hands. This helps disguise the neat cuts made by the scissors.

5. Wait until one of your parents has put a load of washing into the washing machine. When they have turned the machine on and walked away, sneak in and put your item of clothing into the machine.

6. When your parent shows you the torn clothing, get very upset. Try and put on an Academy Award-winning acting performance.

7. When your parent tries to cheer you, mention the item of clothing that you saw in the shop. However, do not mention it too early or they may get suspicious.

Number 60: Yesterday's News

Sometimes today's news seems very similar to yesterday's news. With this joke, today's news is *exactly the same* as yesterday's news.

The Sting

Your mother or father sits down to read the newspaper over breakfast. As they eat their cereal and drink their coffee, they read the front page. Then they read the second page. So far, they're reading the latest news. They go onto the third page, then the fourth page, and so on. The further they get into the newspaper, the more they begin to feel as if they've read it all before. They check the date on the front page, but it's certainly today's newspaper. So they go back to reading. Finally, they come across a story that they are sure they've read before. They check the date on that page. It's yesterday's date. Somehow, the inside pages of the newspaper are from the day before.

What You Need

- an old newspaper (preferably from the day before)

- today's newspaper

The Set-up

1. The day before you are going to play the joke, keep the newspaper after it has been read.

2. If you get the newspaper delivered to your house, get

up nice and early on the day that you are going to play the joke so that you are the first to get to the paper.

3. If someone in your house usually goes to the shop to buy the newspaper, on the day that you are going to play the joke offer to go and buy it.

4. Take all of the inside pages out of today's newspaper. You should be left with the front and back pages, as well as the second and second last pages.

5. Take the inside pages out of yesterday's newspaper and place them inside the front and back pages of today's newspaper.

6. Put the newspaper in its usual place.

7. Sit near your parent as they read the newspaper. See how long it takes them to notice that they're reading yesterday's news.

Number 61: Daylight Saving

Some states and countries turn their clocks forward an hour at the beginning of summer and turn them back again at the end of summer. This is so people can enjoy more sunshine at the end of the day, rather than early in the morning when they are asleep. This joke also involves changing the time on clocks but it has nothing to do with daylight saving.

I've got two minutes to catch my bus... I've got twenty minutes until the board meeting. I've got appointments all day... And I've still got TEDDY BEAR PYJAMAS ON!

The Sting

Your mother or father gets up in the morning to get ready for work. They look at the clock and notice that they have slept in. They have a quicker shower than usual, skip breakfast, race out of the house and rush to work. There seems to be less traffic than normal, which is good because it means they might not be too late for work. When they finally get to work, they find they're the first person there. They check their watch, then look at the clock at work. For some reason their watch is an hour faster than the clock.

What You Need

• all the clocks and watches in the house

The Set-up

1. Wait until your parents have gone to bed and are asleep.

2. Change the time on all the clocks in the house.

3. Also change the time on the your parents' watches. (Be very quiet when you're changing the time on the clocks and watches in your parents' bedroom. You don't want to wake them.)

4. Some clocks are easy to overlook. You'll need to change these as well. These include:

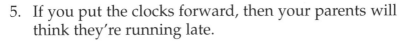

- clocks on video recorders

- clocks on microwave ovens

- clocks on wall ovens

- clocks on computers

- clocks on radios

- clocks in cars

5. If you put the clocks forward, then your parents will think they're running late.

6. If you put the clocks back, then your parents will think they're running early.

7. Do not play this joke if one of your parents has an important meeting to attend. You do not want the joke to cause any major problems.

8. If you only want to cause minor inconvenience, change the time by half an hour instead of an hour.

9. If you have brothers or sisters, tell them about the joke you are playing. That way, they won't spoil the joke by telling your parents the real time.

Number 62: Burnt Toast

In most households the breakfast routine is the same every morning. This is a joke to play on someone who has toast for breakfast every morning. It is particularly good to play on someone who is very fussy about how they like their toast.

The Sting

Your mother or father turns the kettle on to boil water for their cup of tea or coffee. They also put two pieces of bread into the toaster. While their bread is toasting, they leave the kitchen to get their bag ready for work or to put a load of washing into the washing machine. When they return to the kitchen, their toast has popped up but it is burnt. The kitchen is full of smoke and the smoke alarm is ringing. Your parent checks the dial on the toaster but it is on its usual setting. They have no idea how their toast got burnt.

What You Need

- a toaster

The Set-up

1. Make sure that you get into the kitchen before anyone else.

2. Turn the dial on the toaster up so that it will heat the bread for longer than usual.

3. Do not act suspicious when your parent puts their toast in the toaster.

4. If your parent is out of the kitchen when their toast burns, quickly turn the dial back to its usual setting. This will confuse them even more.

5. If your parent stays in the kitchen, run to the toaster to rescue the burning toast. While you are there, quickly turn the dial back to its usual place.

6. Tell your parent that you heard on the radio that bakeries are slicing bread thinner than normal in a bid to put more slices into each packet. That must be the reason their toast burnt.

Similar Joke

- Rather than turning the dial up, you could turn the dial right down, so that the bread hardly toasts at all. When your parent goes to the toaster, they may even wonder whether they pushed the toaster lever down at all.

Number 63: Water Flow

Frustrate your parents while they're watering the garden or washing the car. Their water supply will keep going on and off and they won't know why.

The Sting

One of your parents is watering the garden. They're standing with the hose in their hand, enjoying the peace and quiet. Suddenly the water stops coming out of the hose. Someone must have turned the tap off. They drop the hose and walk to the tap, but no one has touched the tap. Suddenly they hear the water coming out of the hose again. They walk back to the hose and pick it up. Just as they start watering the garden again, the water stops coming out of the hose. This happens four or five times and they never manage to find out why it's happening.

What You Need

- a hose
- the main water-supply tap

The Set-up

1. To do this joke, you have to find the tap that controls the main water supply to your house.

2. If you can operate this tap without being seen by your parent as they water the garden or wash the car, then you can play this joke.

3. Wait until your parent has been watering the garden or

130

washing the car for a couple of minutes, then turn the tap off.

4. The first thing that your parent will probably do is check that the hose is not twisted.

5. The second thing that your parent will probably do is walk to the hose tap and check that it hasn't been turned off.

6. Turn the tap on again after about thirty seconds. Wait another couple of minutes, then turn the tap off again. Repeat this as often as you like.

7. Your parent will probably not think to check the main water tap. However, if you hear them coming your way, turn the tap on and hide. Return to the tap after your parent has checked it and keep playing the joke.

Number 64: Tool Box

If your dad loves fixing things around the house, you can give him a big surprise by playing the Tool Box practical joke.

The Sting

The victim decides it's time they fix that broken chair that has been stored in the corner of the shed for months, ever since it fell apart when your great aunt sat on it. The victim goes into the shed, grabs their tool box and puts the chair on top of the workbench. The first thing they need to do is unscrew the chair legs. They open their tool box and reach for their screwdriver. They find a screwdriver but it's not the one they usually use. It's a plastic screwdriver. Their hammer is also plastic. In fact, every one of their tools has been replaced by a toy tool. The victim looks at the wall of their shed where their saws usually hang. These too have been replaced by plastic saws. Even their power drill is a toy drill.

What You Need

- the victim's tool box

- plastic tools

The Set-up

1. Buy or borrow lots of toy tools.

2. Find out where your victim keeps their tools.

3. When your victim is not around, replace their tools with the toy tools. (Be very careful handling the real tools. Some tools have very sharp edges and points. To be extra safe, wear thick gloves.)

4. Hide the real tools.

5. If your victim shows no sign of wanting to use their tool box, point out that something around the house needs fixing.

Similar Joke

- Rather than replacing the real tools with toy tools, you could hide the real tools around the house, shed and garden, and leave notes in the tool box that offer clues to where the tools can be found.

Number 65:
The Instant Millionaire

Everyone dreams of becoming a millionaire. With this joke, you can make your mother or father believe that they have just become an instant millionaire.

The Sting

Your mother or father is sitting in front of their TV, holding a lotto ticket. The lotto draw is about to begin. The first number drawn is on their ticket. The second number drawn is on their ticket. So are the third, fourth and fifth numbers. Soon, the victim is just one number away from becoming an instant millionaire. The last number is drawn and it matches the one on their ticket. They jump up and down with joy. They believe they have won a million dollars. But they have really just been stung by a practical joke.

What You Need

- a lotto ticket
- a TV set
- a video recorder
- a videotape

The Set-up

1. Videotape the lotto draw from television one night.

2. The following day go out and buy a lotto ticket for the next draw, using the same numbers as the winning draw that you taped.

3. Give the victim the lotto ticket as a present.

4. Just before the lotto draw is usually televised, put the videotape into the video recorder and press 'Play'.

5. Call out to your victim that the lotto draw is on.

6. See your victim's excitement grow as they watch the draw.

7. Do not let your victim celebrate for too long before breaking the bad news.

Sibling Jokes

Sibling jokes are practical jokes that you play on your brothers or sisters. The only problem with playing sibling practical jokes is that your siblings are likely to try and get back at you. Once a 'practical-joke war' has broken out in your household, it is very difficult to stop. However, remember that if you enjoy playing practical jokes on people, you have to be willing to be the victim of a practical joke from time to time.

Number 66: Bath Time

This is a great joke to play on your brother or sister. It works particularly well after they have had a tough day playing sport and are looking forward to a hot, relaxing bath.

The Sting

The victim runs a hot bath. They need it to soothe their tired muscles. When the bath is ready, they get undressed, step into the bath and lie down. The bottom of the bath feels scratchy. They move about in an attempt to get a bit more comfortable. But wherever they settle, it feels uncomfortable. Finally, they

give themselves a quick wash and get out of the bath. It was far from satisfactory. They let the water out and notice a layer of sand on the bottom of the bath.

What You Need

- sand

- a bathtub

- a sibling who is really looking forward to having a bath

The Set-up

1. Buy or collect some sand.
   You don't need much. Hide it in a bag in a secret place.

2. Keep your ears and eyes open so that you know when your brother or sister is looking forward to having a bath.

3. Wait for them to run their bath.

4. While the water's running, they'll probably leave the bathroom. Sneak in and sprinkle the sand into the bath. The sand will sink to the bottom. (Don't sprinkle in too much sand or the victim might notice it when they step into the bath. You want the victim to feel a little bit irritated by the sand while they're lying in the bath. You don't want them to put a foot straight into a pile of wet sand.)

5. Make sure that you're not around when the victim gets out of the bath. They'll probably be in a bad mood.

Similar Joke

- You can play a similar joke by squeezing a lot of bubble bath into the water while the bath is running. Make sure you squirt in a lot so that there are bubbles flowing over the side of the bath when the victim returns to the bathroom.

Number 67: Short Sheet

This joke will irritate your brother and sister just when they least want to be irritated—when they're getting into bed. It's a very common joke and an easy one to play, but it only works on beds with top sheets.

Hey! What's stuck down in my bed? I can't get my legs down. It can't be you Teddy... You're over there!

If you asked me... I'd say someone's short sheeted your bed!

The Sting

The victim is ready for bed. They are in their pyjamas, have cleaned their teeth and have said goodnight to everyone. They turn down the covers on their bed and put their feet under the sheet. The only problem is they can't push their feet down to the bottom of the bed. No matter how hard they push, the sheet won't let them stretch out. They may have been relaxed when they started to get into bed but now they're hopping mad.

What You Need

• five minutes alone in your victim's bedroom

The Set-up

1. Take the top sheet and the blanket or duvet off the bed.

2. Hide the top sheet. You don't need it any more.

3. Undo the bottom sheet from the bottom end of the bed.

4. Fold the sheet in half, so that the both ends are at the top end of the bed.

5. Put the blanket or duvet back on the bed, then fold the top part of the sheet over the top of the blanket or duvet.

6. The sheet should now only go halfway down the bed but, from the outside, everything appears normal.

7. Wait to hear the shouts from the victim.

Special Note

Of course, this joke won't work if your brother or sister never makes their bed. They'll suspect something immediately if they see a neat bed.

Number 68: Wakey, Wakey

Don't play this joke on a brother or sister if you share a bedroom with them. Otherwise, the joke will be on you as well.

The Sting

It's four o'clock in the morning and your brother or sister is sound asleep. They had a late night and they went to bed looking forward to sleeping in. At four o'clock, their alarm clock goes off. It wakes them up. They're so sleepy that they try and think why they set the alarm to go off at four o'clock. They can't think of any reason so they just turn the alarm clock off and go back to sleep. They never do find out why their alarm clock went off.

What You Need

- an alarm clock

- a tired brother or sister

- a torch (for Follow-up)

The Set-up

1. Before your brother or sister goes to bed, sneak into their room.
   (The best time to do this is when they are out with friends, watching their favourite TV show or having a bath or shower. This way it's unlikely you'll be seen.)

2. Set your brother's or sister's alarm clock to go off very early.

Follow-up

- If your brother or sister asks whether you played a joke

on them, say 'No'. If you admit to playing the joke, they may try to get back at you.

- If you think that your brother or sister suspects you, make sure that you check your alarm clock before you go to sleep. They may try to play the same trick on you.

- If you are willing to get up early, you can continue the joke. Set your alarm to go off at the same time as your brother's or sister's alarm. Allow your brother or sister about fifteen minutes to get back to sleep, then sneak into their room. You may need a torch to see what you're doing. Set their alarm to go off again in an hour's time. Repeat this throughout the morning for as long as you think you can get away with it.

Number 69:
A Stitch in Time

This joke requires you to do a bit of sewing. You don't have to be a neat sewer because the victim will want to unpick your work straight away.

The Sting

Your brother or sister has a big game today. They've been looking forward to it since last weekend. They get their sports uniform out of the cupboard and begin thinking about the game. They're feeling happy because they reckon today they'll be voted Most Valuable Player and will win the game for their team. They put their shirt on and try to put their arms through the sleeves. But their arms won't go through. The sleeves have been stitched together. They throw the shirt to the ground and put their trousers on. But their feet won't go through. The legs of the trousers have been stitched up as well. Now they're not thinking about being Most Valuable Player. They're too busy ripping the stitches out.

What You Need

- a needle and thread

- your victim's sports uniform

The Set-up

1. When your brother or sister is out, go to their room and find their sports uniform.

2. Using the needle and thread, sew up the end of one of the sleeves.

3. Sew up the end of the other sleeve.

4. Sew up the end of one of the legs.

5. Sew up the end of the other leg.

6. Put the uniform back where you found it.

7. It doesn't have to be their sports uniform that you sew up. You could sew up the ends of their pyjamas or their school uniform. However, make sure that you don't sew up any new or expensive clothes.

Follow-up

- If your brother or sister plays a team sport and it is your household's turn to wash all the uniforms, why not get a couple of friends to help you sew up the ends of all the uniforms. It will be a very funny scene when all the uniforms are handed out at the sports ground.

Number 70: Sew-Sew

Here is another practical joke that involves sewing.

The Sting

Your brother or sister is getting ready to go out with friends. They open a drawer to choose a shirt to wear. They find the red shirt they want and pull it out. But it's not just the red shirt that comes out. They also pull out a blue shirt, a white shirt, a black shirt and a green shirt. All of the shirts in the drawer have been sewn together. They open their underwear drawer and find that all of their underwear has been sewn together, too. So have their socks. It doesn't stop them going out for the night, but they do have to undo the stitches before they can get dressed.

What You Need

- a needle and thread
- your victim's clothes
- a couple of hours to carry out the joke

The Set-up

1. When your victim is out of the house, go to their chest of drawers.

2. Take all of your victim's clothes out of one drawer.

3. Take two items of clothing and sew them together. It doesn't matter if you sew them together at the cuffs, legs or waists.

4. Repeat this process until all the clothing from the drawer is sewn together. Put the clothes back.

5. Take the clothes from another drawer, sew them together as well. Put them back.

Hmmm...Hard to believe... someone's turned my drawer into a washing line!

6. You can sew together the clothes from as many drawers as you like.

7. Pick up any loose threads and needles. Otherwise the victim may spot them and get suspicious before they open their drawers.

Set-up Tips

• You don't have to do too much sewing, just a couple of stitches to join the clothing together. You don't want to make it too hard for the victim to unpick the stitches.

• Do not sew any new or expensive clothes together. You do not want to damage them.

Number 71: A Trip to the Shops

This joke is played on a younger brother or sister. It involves sending them to the shops, even though you know they will be coming back empty-handed.

The Sting

Your younger brother or sister goes to the shops with special instructions from you. They are on the hunt for a left-handed screwdriver. They try three stores, with no luck. All they get are laughs from the shopkeepers. In the end, they return home without the screwdriver. That's because there is no such thing as a left-handed screwdriver. Unless you tell them, they may never know they have been the victim of a practical joke.

What You Need

• a victim likely to believe your request

The Set-up

1. Pretend to be doing some work around the house.

2. Call your brother or sister and ask if they'll run to the shop and buy something for you. Tell them you'd go yourself but you're busy doing a job. If they complain, tell them you'll give them some money when they come back with the correct goods.

3. Ask them to buy a left-handed screwdriver, or think of

another item that sounds real but does not exist. Here are a few examples:

- a metric hammer
- a tin of striped paint
- a tin of spotted paint
- smooth sandpaper
- a straight hook
- invisible ink

4. When the victim returns empty-handed, it's up to you to decide whether to tell them that you've played a practical joke on them.

Similar Joke

- A similar joke involves letting a particular shopkeeper know in advance that you're going to play a practical joke. You then send your brother or sister to that shop with instructions to buy 'a long weight'. Write 'a long weight' down on a piece of paper, rather than say it, otherwise they might realise what the joke is. When they get to the shop, they will say 'Can I have a long weight?'. The shopkeeper will then keep them waiting. When your brother or sister complains, the shopkeeper will say, 'I'm giving you the long wait you asked for'.

Number 72: Mirror, Mirror on the Wall

Snow White looked in the mirror and was told she was the fairest of all. When your brother or sister looks in the mirror, they will certainly not be the fairest of all.

The Sting

You tell your brother or sister they have strange spots on their face. The victim does not believe you. You tell them you are not joking. Still they do not believe you. In the end, you go and fetch a mirror so they can see for themselves. When you come back with the mirror, you hold it up in front of their face. They get the shock of their life when they see that you are right. Their face is covered with spots.

What You Need

- a portable mirror
- a felt pen

The Set-up

1. Find a portable mirror that is large enough to show someone's full face.

2. Using the felt pen, put a few spots on the mirror. Make sure that you put the spots where someone's face will appear. To do this, hold the mirror in front of your face at about the same distance that you will hold it from the victim's face.

3. Rather than come out straight away and tell the victim that they have spots on their face, give them a couple of strange looks. When they ask you 'What's wrong?', tell them 'There's nothing wrong'. Then wait a minute and give them another strange look. This time, when they ask 'What's wrong?', tell them they have spots on their face.

4. When they say they don't believe you, or if they get up to have a look, offer to get a mirror for them. Get up and fetch the mirror before they have a chance to get to another mirror first.

5. Carry the mirror so that the victim cannot see the front of it.

6. When you hold the mirror up in front of their face, make sure you keep it very still. Otherwise the spots will move and the victim will become suspicious.

Number 73:
Change the Channel

Some brothers and sisters spend a lot of time arguing about which TV program they're going to watch. When this happens, the remote control is a very important weapon.

The Sting

You are watching a TV program when your brother or sister joins you. They do not like the program you are watching and start complaining about it. You tell them to be quiet and let you watch the program in peace. They reach for the remote control and press the button for the channel they want to watch. Nothing happens. They press the button a bit harder. Still nothing happens. They start pressing all the buttons, one after the other. Still nothing happens. You laugh to yourself as you happily watch your favourite TV program to the very end. Your victim gets so frustrated that they storm off to their room, leaving you to watch whatever you like for the whole night.

What You Need

- a TV remote control

- a TV set

The Set-up

1. Set the TV to the channel you want to watch.

2. Take the batteries out of the remote control.

3. Hide the batteries.

4. Hide any other batteries that fit the remote control.

5. Put the remote control in its usual place, then sit back and wait for the fun to start.

Similar Joke

- If you really want to drive someone mad, reprogram the remote control so that the buttons no longer relate to the right channels. To do this, you'll need half an hour alone with the remote control. If there's one particular channel that you know the victim does not like, reprogram every button so that they all control that channel.

Number 74: Shaving Cream

Play this joke when your brother or sister is in their room relaxing. It will certainly get their attention.

The Sting

Your victim is in their bedroom listening to some music and reading a book. They just want a bit of peace and quiet. Before settling down with their book, they cleaned their room. Everything is neat and tidy. They are so caught up in their reading and music that they don't hear or see something being slipped under their door. A moment later, their peace and quiet is totally ruined when shaving cream flies through the air and lands all over their bed, their clothes, their desk and just about everywhere else in their room. Even their book is covered with shaving cream.

What You Need

- a large envelope
- a can of shaving cream
- a closed door

The Set-up

1. Wait until the victim is alone in their room with the door closed.

2. Open the envelope and squirt it full of shaving cream. Do not seal the envelope.

3. Quietly sneak up to the closed door.

4. Place the open end of the envelope under the door so that it is sticking out the other side.

5. Jump on top of the half of the envelope that contains the shaving cream.

6. The shaving cream will explode out of the open end of the envelope and will end up all over the victim's room.

Number 75: Smaller and Smaller

Sometimes objects appear smaller than you remember. In this joke, the change in size is not an illusion, it's real.

The Sting

Your sister is in her bedroom polishing the jewellery box that you gave her for her birthday. You made the box yourself. A few days later, she again polishes the jewellery box. She looks inside and thinks the jewellery is a bit more cramped than usual. A few days later, your sister opens the box again to get a piece of jewellery out. The jewellery seems even more cramped than the last time she looked. She closes the box and looks at it from the outside. It seems a bit smaller than she remembered. Over the next few days, the box appears to get even smaller. Your sister is very confused. Then, over the next couple of weeks, the box seems to increase in size. She makes an appointment to get her eyes tested.

Oh dear! How do I get a set of plastic earrings, an imitation pearl necklace with a fake diamond and a very large throwaway watch into such a small jewellery box?

What You Need

- a series of identical-looking items (all a slightly different size)

The Set-up

1. Make or buy a number of identical-looking items that are all a slightly different size.

2. Give the largest item to your brother or sister as a present. Tell them that it has magical qualities.

3. A few days later, replace the original item with the one a size smaller.

4. Repeat the process every few days, using a slightly smaller item each time.

5. Once you have reached the smallest item, gradually replace the items in increasing size.

6. You can go down and up in size as long as you like. If your victim ever says something to you, remind them that you said the item had magical qualities.

Similar Joke

• If your brother or sister has a poster or picture with a wide border, you can make the poster or picture appear to be getting smaller by trimming the border a little bit every few days. However, do not do this with a valuable painting.

Jokes on Your Parents' Visitors

Do you ever feel the urge to play a practical joke on your parents' friends? It's hard not to get the urge to play a joke when you hear them laughing and yelling around the dinner table. Well, here's your chance to get back at them for all the times their noise has kept you awake.

Number 76: Raining Confetti

There have been many songs written about rain, such as 'Raindrops Keep Falling on My Head' and 'It's Raining Men'. I've never heard one about raining confetti but that's what this joke is about.

The Sting

After a great party at your house, your parents' friends get ready to go home. It was raining when they arrived so many of them brought umbrellas. As they step outside, they put their umbrellas up. They get the shock of their lives when hundreds of tiny pieces of confetti rain down on their heads.

What You Need

- confetti
- the victims' umbrellas

The Set-up

1. This trick can only be done on a rainy night. As your parents' guests arrive, watch to see if any of them brought an umbrella. If they did, then you can begin preparing the joke.

2. Wait until all your parents' guests are having dinner, watching a movie or busy doing something else.

3. Open the end of each umbrella and pour lots of confetti inside.

4. Close each umbrella back up.

5. Clean up any confetti that you may have dropped. You don't want anyone getting suspicious.

6. If you can, stay awake so that you can watch out of the window as it starts raining confetti.

Similar Jokes

There are a number of other objects that you can put inside an umbrella. Here's a few suggestions:

- an egg (so that it splatters on the ground)

- ping-pong balls (so that they bounce off the victim's head and then all over the ground)

- a pile of flour (so that the victim's hair turns white)

Number 77: Whoopee

Whoopee cushions are one of the most popular items in practical-joke shops. One whoopee cushion can cause embarrassment to many, many people. Try a whoopee cushion next time your parents have visitors over.

The Sting

Oh Mr. Jones! Was it something you ate?
Is it indigestion?
Do you have a medical problem?
OR WAS IT SOMETHING YOU SAT ON? Hee Hee!
BBRRARR

Some of your parents' friends have come over for dinner. They are standing around talking before dinner is served. One of them decides to sit down on the sofa. They walk over and take a seat. The moment their bottom hits the cushion, a loud sound breaks out. It sounds like someone breaking wind. Everybody turns to look at the victim who has turned red with embarrassment.

What You Need

- a whoopee cushion

- a sofa or chair with cushions

The Set-up

1. Buy a whoopee cushion from a joke or magic shop.

2. Blow some air into the cushion. You do not need to blow the cushion all the way up. If it is too full, you may not be able to hide it under a sofa cushion.

3. Just before your parents' friends come over, place the cushion under a sofa cushion.

4. Hide where you can see the sofa but where you cannot be seen.

5. Wait for the fun to begin.

Similar Joke

- You don't have to place the whoopee cushion on a chair or sofa to make the joke work. Try hiding under the dinner table and place the whoopee cushion under your arm. As each person sits down, press your arm down so that the whoopee cushion makes its noise. The only problem is escaping from under the table without being seen.

Number 78: The Stirrer

You can play this joke whenever one of your parents' friends pops in for a cup of tea or coffee. But don't play it on the same person twice or they'll get suspicious.

The Sting

The victim accepts your offer of a cup of coffee. You bring them their cup and teaspoon, as well as the milk and sugar. The victim adds a bit of milk to the coffee, then takes the teaspoon and spoons some sugar into the cup. They then stir their coffee. When they take the teaspoon out, they're left with only the handle—the bottom part has fallen off. They have no idea how it happened, but they feel very embarrassed.

What You Need

- an old teaspoon
- some chewing gum
- a hot cup of tea or coffee

Oh my! Doris... this is TEA that we're drinking isn't it? I've just lost the end of my spoon in my cup!

The Set-up

1. Buy an old teaspoon from a second-hand shop or use an old one from home. Make sure you don't use a valuable teaspoon or someone's favourite spoon because you are going to destroy it.

2. Grab the oval end of the teaspoon with one hand and hold the handle tightly with the other hand.

3. Wiggle the oval end until you feel it loosening. It will eventually break off.

4. When it has broken off, get a tiny piece of chewing gum and stick the two pieces back together. Make sure that

the gum cannot be seen. You only need enough to stop the spoon breaking when it is picked up.

5. Give the victim the spoon with their hot drink. It has to be a hot drink because the heat will melt the gum.

6. As the victim stirs sugar or milk into their drink, tell them that the spoon is your favourite because it was given to you by a very special friend. This will make them feel even worse when it breaks.

Similar Joke

- You can play this joke on a whole heap of people at once. If you know that your parents are going to host a dinner party, prepare several spoons in the way described above and make sure that they are set out on the table with the coffee and tea.

Number 79: Moving Objects

This joke makes people go to the optometrist to get their eyes tested. If you play this joke well, people will think they're seeing things.

The Sting

Your parents have a number of friends over for dinner. Before dinner, they sit around the living room chatting. One of them thinks they see a small ceramic figure move a little bit to the left. A bit later, someone thinks they see an empty chair move backwards a little bit. When everyone is sitting around having dinner, other people see various objects move ever so slightly. No one says anything because they're worried that the others will think they're mad (or that they've had too much to drink).

What You Need

- fishing line

- lots of objects

The Set-up

1. Buy a reel of fishing line. You'll need quite a lot of it.

2. Find out which room your parents' visitors will be using.

3. Choose a number of objects in that room that you can move. Do not choose fragile objects that will break if they fall.

4. The objects must have a part that a piece of fishing line can be tied to.

5. Cut the fishing line into as many pieces as you need.

6. Tie one piece of fishing line to each object.

7. Run the fishing line to a place where you will be able to sit without being seen.

8. Make sure the fishing line is not visible. Run it under rugs, next to walls and across mantelpieces.

9. When the guests have arrived, get into your hiding place and every now and again give one of the lines a small tug. Do not pull too hard. You don't want to make the movement too obvious.

10. Enjoy the look on the faces of the visitors who think they are seeing things.

Number 80:
One Down, All Down

This joke is bit like a game of tenpin bowling. When one victim goes down, others follow.

The Sting

Your parents are hosting a dinner party. All is going well. Everyone is sitting around the dinner table having a great time. Finally, the dessert is finished and the plates have been cleared. Everyone sits around the table for a bit longer before one of your parents suggests they all move to the living room. The visitors all stand up and start to move. As soon as one moves, they topple over and fall to the ground. The person next to them also falls, as does the next person and the next person and the next person. Soon, every guest is lying on the floor.

The Set-up

1. Hide under the dinner table before everyone sits down or sneak under the table without being seen after everyone is seated.

Oh boy! I think...

I'M GOING TO FALL OVER!

Oh dear... So am I

Me too...! I think the goose liver pate might have been off!

2. While everyone is eating, very carefully move from one visitor to the next, undoing their shoelaces and tying them to their neighbour's.

3. If one of the visitors is wearing shoes with straps rather than shoes with laces, try tying the lace of the person next to them to the side of the strap. If you can't do this

without being noticed, then just move to the next person with laces and start again.

4. When you have worked your way around the whole table, sneak away.

5. Hide where you can see the visitors fall when they all stand up.

Similar Joke

- Instead of tying everyone's shoelaces together, you could tie the visitors' shoelaces to the chair legs or even to the table legs.

Safety Tip

- Don't play this joke on pregnant women, old people, frail people, or people with injuries. You don't want to hurt anyone.

Uncle Bob   Nana   Aunt Patty
The
SCENE UNDER THE TABLE
AT MUM and DAD'S DINNER PARTY

Sport, Entertainment and Art Jokes

This chapter contains practical jokes that can be played at sports, entertainment and arts events. Some of them can be played by participants, others by spectators.

Number 81: No Ball

This practical joke works well in a game of baseball, softball or cricket. It could also be adapted to be used in a game of tennis. This joke is best played on someone who boasts about how good a sportsperson they are. The victim of the joke will probably end up getting their eyes checked.

The Sting

Your victim holds the bat in their hands. They are one of the best players on their team and have often scored the winning run. The pitcher or bowler releases the ball. The catcher or wicketkeeper yells and raises their hands. They claim they've caught the ball after it hit the bat. The victim did not even see the ball approach and is certain that it did not hit their bat. However, the umpire also says that the ball was caught after hitting the bat. The umpire tells the victim that they are out.

What You Need

- a catcher or wicketkeeper who knows about the joke

- an umpire who knows about the joke

The Set-up

1. Tell the catcher or wicketkeeper about the joke. Agree on a secret signal that you can give when you, as pitcher or bowler, are going to play the joke.

2. Tell the umpire about the joke. Tell them about the secret signal so they know when the joke is going to take place.

3. You could also tell other members of your team (and even members of the other team if you think they will appreciate the joke).

4. When the time comes and you are pitching or bowling, give the secret signal.

5. Take your stance or start your run-up.

6. Do not change your pitching or bowling action. The only difference with this pitch or bowl is that you don't release the ball.

7. When the pitcher or wicketkeeper jumps up and down, you should also get excited.

8. Turn to the umpire as if awaiting their decision.

9. Celebrate when the umpire declares that the victim has been fairly caught or struck out.

Follow-up

- In the spirit of fair play, the victim should be told about the joke shortly after they have left the field. They should then be asked to take their place on the field again. If you promise to do this, you are more likely to get the agreement of the victim's team to join in with the joke.

Number 82: The Artwork

This practical joke is played at an art exhibition. It could be an art exhibition at your school or a larger, public exhibition.

The Sting

It is the opening of an art exhibition and art lovers are walking around studying the exhibits. They come across a very strange one. It is a blank piece of paper with an ink spot on it. You and a friend are standing in front of this work discussing how good it is and what you think it represents. Gradually, other people also start discussing it. They all have their own ideas of what the painting means. You and your friend stand back and have fun watching and listening to these so-called art experts. The reason for your amusement is that the painting they are discussing was done by you and secretly taped to the wall.

What You Need

- a painting
- some adhesive tape
- a label
- a friend to help with the joke

The Set-up

1. Paint a simple picture. The idea of this joke is to get people discussing a work of art that you know has no meaning whatsoever. Here are a few suggestions:

- an ink spot on white paper
- a piece of paper with a single piece of string hanging off it
- a piece of paper with two stripes painted on it
- a crumpled piece of paper glued to a piece of paper of a different colour

2. Give your work of art a title and write this on the label. The name should be as unusual as the artwork.

3. Make up the name of an artist and write this on the label as well.

4. Take your picture, label and some tape to an art show.

5. When you are alone in the room, quickly tape the painting and label to the wall near some other pictures. Your friend can act as lookout.

6. Stand in front of your painting and wait for some people to enter the room. As they walk past, start discussing your work of art with your friend. Talk loudly so that people can hear you. Before long, you'll have many people discussing your work.

Number 83:
Wrong Colours

This is a fun practical joke that can be played at almost any sports event. Try it next time your school is playing another school in football, basketball or any other sport.

The Sting

The victim is sitting among a large group of people who are all cheering for the same team. They shout very loudly for the 'Reds'. Suddenly, when there is a moment of quiet, a shout of 'Go Blues' comes from the seat of the victim. Everyone stares and starts shouting at the victim. The victim claims they didn't say anything, but the next time it goes quiet, the same shout comes from the victim's seat. Later, the victim seems to shout 'The Blues are Best' and 'Blues, Blues, Blues'. By now, the victim is very unpopular with the Reds supporters.

What You Need

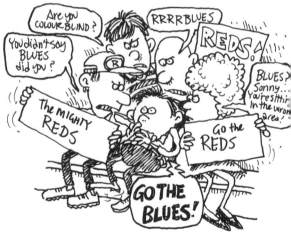

- a portable tape recorder

- a blank audiotape (for recording shouts)

- a sporting event

The Set-up

1. Decide which sporting event you are going to attend with the victim.

2. During the week, put the blank audiotape in the tape recorder and record shouts for the team that you and the victim do not support. Make the shouts different from each other.

3. On the day of the sporting event, hide the tape recorder in a bag so that the victim doesn't know you have it.

4. At the sporting event, make sure you sit among people supporting the same team as you.

5. When the victim goes to the toilet or to buy something to eat, take the tape recorder out of your bag, turn the volume right up, and place it under or behind the victim's seat.

6. Make sure that you can press the 'Play' button. It you place the tape recorder behind the victim, you can lean over and press it. If you put the tape recorder under the victim's chair, you may have to take off a shoe and sock and press it with your toe. You might want to practise this at home.

7. When there is a quiet moment, press the 'Play' button, so that the tape recorder plays a shout for the opposing team. Look at the victim in disgust. Other people will probably do the same.

8. Repeat this every now and again during the match.

Transport Jokes

The jokes in this chapter involve various forms of transport, such as bicycles, cars, even a motorbike with a sidecar. Sometimes the person riding or driving the vehicle is the victim. Other times the rider or driver is carrying out the joke. It is important to remember that practical jokes involving transport must not put anyone at risk of having an accident.

Number 84: Rattle, Rattle, Rattle

This joke is not dangerous but is extremely irritating to the victim. It is a great joke because it can go on for days or even weeks.

The Sting

The victim gets in their car, starts it up and drives away. Before long they hear a rattling sound. They have no idea what it is, but they stop the car, get out and have a good look. They find nothing wrong and get back into the car. As soon as they drive away, the

rattling starts again. This goes on for as long as it takes the victim to discover the stones that have been placed in the car's hub-caps.

What You Need

- the victim's car
- small stones
- a large screwdriver
- a hammer

Hey! Nice new car! Shame about that horrible sound it's making! Maybe it's a loose bolt in your overhead cam.. A blown gasket in the turbo perhaps. A worn steering coupling? Boy! Whatever it is ... it sounds AWFUL!

The Set-up

1. Make sure that your victim will be away from their car for at least ten minutes.

2. Place the sharp end of the screwdriver underneath the edge of a hub-cap and lever the hub-cap off.

3. Place some stones inside the hub-cap.

4. Position the hub-cap back in place, then tap it with the hammer until you are sure it is on properly.

5. Repeat the process with the other three hub-caps.

Set-up Tips

- Practise removing and replacing hub-caps on cars at your home first. That way you'll know how much time you'll need.

- Be careful not to damage the car tyres with the screwdriver.

- The size of the stones is important. They should not be so small that they'll fall through gaps between the hub-caps and tyres. However, they should not be so large that the force of them knocking against a hub-cap will cause the hub-cap to fly off.

- Try and be a passenger in the car after playing the joke. It is great fun witnessing the victim's confusion.

Number 85: All in Order

It is amazing that this joke works because it seems so silly. However, you'll be surprised how easily people are fooled.

The Sting

The victim skates towards you on their skateboard. You yell something and gesture towards the back of their skateboard. They stop and check their skateboard, before realising they've been the butt of a joke. After all, you didn't say that anything was wrong.

What You Need

- nothing, just a victim with a skateboard

The Set-up

1. As the victim skateboards towards you, gesture towards the back of their skateboard and yell out, 'Your back wheels are going round'.

2. You haven't told the victim that something is wrong. In fact you're telling them that everything is OK. However, the way that you gesture and the tone of your voice suggests that there is a problem.

3. Stand back and watch the victim as they get off their skateboard and check that everything is OK. When they realise that there is no problem, they'll probably think back and remember what you said. Then they'll realise they've been the victim of a practical joke.

Similar Jokes

- For people cycling past on a bicycle, you can call out,

'Your back wheel is going around' or 'Your pedals are turning'.

- For joggers or walkers going past, you can point to their shoes and call out, 'Your shoelaces are done up'.

- For people driving cars or riding motorbikes, you can call out, 'You've got exhaust coming out of the back' or 'Your engine is working'.

Number 86:
The Still Sidecar

For those of you that have access to a motorbike and sidecar, as well as a motorbike rider, this is a fun joke to play. This joke featured in a film called *Duck Soup* way back in 1933. The film starred a group of famous comedians called the Marx Brothers.

The Sting

The victim is offered a ride in a sidecar that's connected to a motorbike. They climb into the sidecar, put on a helmet and gloves, and get ready for the ride of their life. The motorbike rider starts the bike's engine, makes sure the road is clear, and takes off, leaving the sidecar on the side of the road, with the victim sitting inside it feeling embarrassed.

What You Need

- a motorbike

- a motorbike sidecar

- a spare helmet and gloves

- bricks or blocks of wood

- a motorbike rider

The Set-up

1. On a day the victim is coming to visit, set up the motorbike and sidecar in front of your house.

2. The motorbike and sidecar must look as if they are connected but must really be separate. You may need to place bricks or blocks of wood underneath the sidecar so that it will support a passenger without the bike.

3. When the victim arrives and sees the motorbike and sidecar, introduce the victim to the rider.

4. Tell the victim about the great ride you had in the sidecar last week. When you have finished talking about it, the rider should offer the victim a ride.

5. If the victim is unsure, do your best to convince them.

6. Help the victim into their helmet and gloves and get them settled in the sidecar. Tell them they have to hold on tight when the bike takes off.

7. Stand back and watch their embarrassment when the bike takes off without them.

Follow-up

- If you want to add to the joke, have a grown-up dressed as a police officer walk past the sidecar shortly after the bike takes off. Get them to write out a ticket for illegal parking and give it to the victim. The ticket could have the words 'You've been had' written on it.

Number 87: The Still Trailer

This joke is similar to the Still Sidecar but involves a car and a trailer instead of a motorbike and sidecar. It is an ideal joke to play on someone you are taking to the airport or taking on holiday with you.

The Sting

The victim's luggage is placed on a trailer behind the car. They are asked to help tie the luggage down with rope, straps and anything else you can think of. The driver of the car tells the victim that the trailer has been playing up a bit lately and that they want to make sure that the luggage is safe. The victim gets into the car. The car moves off and, to the victim's horror, the trailer stays behind. The driver is too busy listening to the radio to hear the victim's shouts and the other passengers are busy talking to each other.

What You Need

- a car

- a trailer

- rope, tape or straps

- bricks or blocks of wood

- a driver

The Set-up

1. On a day the victim is going away, set up the car and trailer in front of your house.

2. The car and trailer must look as if they are connected but must really be separate. You may need to place bricks or blocks of wood underneath the trailer so that it will not fall down when filled with luggage.

3. Have the car boot full of other stuff so that it is easy to explain why the trailer is needed.

4. When the victim arrives, put the luggage in the trailer. Ask the victim to help tie the luggage down. Explain that there have been problems with the trailer.

5. Give the victim a seat in the back of the car so that they can see the trailer. If you have told a good enough story about the problems you have been having with the trailer, they will almost certainly keep an eye on it. If they are not watching the trailer, remind them to keep an eye on it.

6. Drive off, leaving the trailer behind.

7. When the victim starts kicking up a fuss about their luggage being left behind, prolong their agony by pretending not to hear them as you listen to the radio or chat with others in the car.

Follow-up

- You can prolong the joke by having someone standing near the trailer but out of sight. As the car goes out of view, get them to remove the luggage and hide it. When the car returns after finally being alerted by the victim, their luggage will be gone.

We'll have to go back for all of my gear. I can't go to the Himalayas without it! Besides... I've got those twenty sherpas waiting in the foothills to carry it all for me!

Number 88: Bus Stop

Gee! What sort of bus ticket did you buy to get all of that? FIRST CLASS? BUSINESS CLASS? I must be travelling ECONOMY. All I got was the ride!

This joke doesn't have a victim but it certainly makes the other passengers take notice and gives them something to talk about at work and school. The joke is ideal for a group of drama students.

The Sting

On morning, you get on a bus (or tram or train) and sit down. At the next stop, someone gets on and hands you a tray with the morning newspaper on it. At the next stop, someone gets on with a glass of juice for you. At the next stop, someone gets on with a bowl of cereal for you. At the next stop, someone gets on with a plate of bacon and eggs for you. By now, the other passengers are staring at you and waiting to see who will get on at the next stop. At the second last stop, someone gets on, wipes your hands and face and takes your tray away. At your last stop, you stand up and get off, as if this happens to you every morning.

What You Need

- lots of volunteers
- a tray
- the morning newspaper
- plates and cutlery
- food and drink
- a cloth or face washer

The Set-up

1. Work out which person is going to get on at which stop and with which props.

2. Make sure everyone has a copy of the timetable and knows which bus (or tram or train) you are going to be on.

3. The actors should also know exactly where you are going to be sitting.

4. Start the journey and try to blend in with the other passengers.

5. As each actor gets on with some food for you, act as if it is the most natural thing in the world to be served breakfast on public transport. The actors must also be as natural as possible.

Set-up Tips

- This practical joke requires the participants to be good actors. The joke works best if everyone acts as if what they are doing is perfectly normal.

- Once the participants have handed you their goods, they should walk away and leave you alone.

- You can add to the joke by getting on the bus in your pyjamas and dressing gown and having some people bring you your clothes during the trip. You can put these clothes on over your pyjamas.

Number 89: Parking Ticket

Parking Ticket is a joke to play on people with cars. It is particularly amusing if you can be near the victim when they find what they think is a parking ticket.

The Sting

The victim parks their car in a two-hour parking spot. They go off to do some shopping and return after an hour. They put the shopping into the boot of their car and walk around to the front. They stop in horror when they see a parking ticket on their windscreen. They check the words on the parking sign, then check their watch. They can't understand how they got a ticket. By now, they are pretty angry. They rip the ticket off their windscreen and open it up to see how much they have been fined. The ticket reads 'Thank you for parking legally. Have a nice day'.

What You Need

WHAT? A PARKING TICKET? But I only turned around for two seconds to put money in the parking meter.

- coloured paper
- sticky tape
- a sheet of plastic
- a parking ticket

The Set-up

1. Have a look at a parking ticket. If someone in your family gets one, ask to have a look. If you can't get hold of a parking ticket, walk down the street and see if you can spot a car with a parking ticket. Don't touch it, but notice what colour it is, what size it is, and how it is folded and taped to the windscreen.

2. Buy some paper the same colour as the parking ticket.

Cut it to size and write a message on it. The message should let the driver know they have been the victim of a practical joke.

3. Fold the paper to the right size.

4. You may want to wrap the ticket in plastic before taping it to a windscreen.

5. Go to a busy street where there are parking restrictions and put the ticket on the windscreen of a parked car. Make sure the driver does not see you.

6. Wait nearby and watch the reaction of the victim when they return to their car. Most people are pretty angry when they get a parking ticket, especially when they know they have done nothing wrong.

7. Watch if their reaction changes when they read the message you wrote.

I'll have to be more careful where I park! You can't take your eyes off your car for a second around here!

Animal Jokes

If you are using real animals in practical jokes, make sure that you never, ever hurt them. A practical joke is not funny if an animal or a person gets hurt.

Number 90:
Spider on the Loose

This joke takes a few days to set up, but it will strike fear into the hearts of many people.

The Sting

All your classmates know that you've got a big, hairy spider in a jar. They know this because you've shown them. Some of your classmates are scared of the spider, others say they're not scared at all. But when you produce the glass jar and it's empty, even those that claimed they weren't scared of spiders will probably jump on top of the nearest desk to escape from a spider on the loose.

What You Need

- a spider (the bigger and hairier the better)

- a jar with a lid, pierced with tiny holes

- some food for the spider (such as ants, flies or other insects)

Can I interest anyone in my very large black hairy spider with eight very hairy legs and twenty eyes? He doesn't bite! Well.. not much!

184

The Set-up

1. Catch a spider and put it in a jar. Be very careful when you're doing this. Make sure you identify the spider first. Do not go anywhere near a spider that may be venomous. (The spider should be as hairy and scary as possible. Your aim is to scare people. You won't be able to scare people with a tiny, cute-looking spider.)

2. Place some food for the spider inside the jar. Ants or flies are good. The spider may be in the jar for a few days.

3. Take the jar to school and show the spider to your friends. Do this two or three days in a row.

4. On the third or fourth day, set the spider free but don't let your friends see you do this.

5. When you're with a large group of friends, bring the jar out as if you're going to show them the spider again. React with horror when you see the jar is empty. Pretend that you can see the spider running around on the ground. Then watch with amusement as your friends run for their lives.

RUN FOR YOUR LIVES! EVACUATE THE BUILDING! MY SPIDER'S ON THE LOOSE!

Now that was an award winning performance if I ever saw one!

Number 91: Moth Attack

Moths are attracted to light. Knowing this means you can play this joke at school or at home.

The Sting

Your teacher has planned a special class. You are going to see some slides. Your teacher turns the main light off and switches the projector on. The students pay attention to the screen as the teacher describes the slides. Suddenly something flickers across the screen. It happens again. And again. There are moths loose in the room and they are fluttering about the projector light. Their shadows appear on the screen, causing several students to shriek with fright. The teacher has to give up on the lesson.

I'm sorry students... Todays film will need to be postponed due to an unforseen moth plague in the theatrette... maybe the film attracted them!

What You Need

- a shoebox
- moths
- a dark room with a single light source

The Set-up

1. The day before carrying out this joke, collect some moths. The best way to collect moths is with a net.

2. Keep the moths in a cardboard box, with small holes in the lid, so that they won't die.

3. Take the box of moths to school. Keep the box hidden until the slideshow has been going for a few minutes.

4. When everyone is distracted by what they are watching, take the lid off the box and watch the moths fly straight to the light.

I'll put enough moths in this box to make Dad's boring slide night a real night to remember!

Similar Jokes

- If your parents are in the habit of holding a slide night after returning from a holiday, then you could liven their show up with this joke. Some of your parents' guests may welcome the distraction.

- If you have a brother or sister who studies at their desk late at night, sneak into their room when they go to the bathroom or kitchen and set some moths free. When your brother or sister returns, they will find a swarm of moths flying around their desk lamp.

Number 92: Fly Away

The creatures in this joke aren't real, but the victim certainly thinks they are.

There are flies in the butter... in the jam... in the sugar! There are flies everywhere. Everywhere except in AAHRRR they're in here too!

The Sting

The victim decides to make a sandwich. They get out the bread, butter and jam. When they open the butter container, they see a fly sitting on the butter. They decide to do without butter and just have the jam. But when they open the jam jar, there is a fly in there as well. Yuk! They check the sugar bowl. A fly is in there. There's also a fly in the fruit bowl and another on the kitchen bench. Thinking that there must be a fly plague, they run to the store to get some fly spray.

What You Need

- plastic flies
- enough time to plant the flies in the victim's kitchen

The Set-up

1. Buy some plastic flies. You can get them at a joke or magic shop. (Never use dead flies for this joke because even dead flies carry lots of germs. You don't want to make anyone sick.)

2. When the victim is out of their kitchen, sneak in and put the flies in different places. It's best to place them on food items because the victim will feel ill when they find them.

3. Place several flies in the sugar bowl. Every time the victim reaches for the sugar over the next few weeks, they won't be able to get the image of the flies out of their mind.

4. Hide somewhere near the kitchen so that you can see or hear the victim's reaction.

Follow-up

- If you want to really turn your victim's stomach, walk into the kitchen soon after they have discovered the flies. Tell the victim that you heard on the radio that flies are very nutritious. Then grab one and pop it in your mouth. Pretend to chew it, but make sure you don't really swallow the plastic fly.

Scary and Sick Jokes

Scary practical jokes involving sheets, torches, shadows, fake blood and strange noises have been played on people for hundreds of years. The best time to play scary practical jokes is at night. This is when your victims are likely to be scared the most. Sick jokes are bad-taste jokes. They are also lots of fun to play.

Number 93: Ghost Story

Hearing a ghost story can be scary enough. Imagine how scary it can be if ghosts seem to appear.

The Sting

A group of your friends are sitting around while you tell a ghost story. The story is frightening, and every now and again strange sounds can be heard. At first, these sounds are very faint and no one says anything because they think they might be imagining it. However, when furniture starts to move, everyone starts screaming. Only you know the truth. You have to decide whether to let your friends in on the joke or let them believe they really saw and heard ghosts.

What You Need

- friends to help you carry out the joke

- pebbles
- torches
- fishing line
- a tape recorder
- a blank audiotape

The Set-up

The planning for this joke
starts well before you begin
telling your ghost story. You have to organise one group of
friends to play a few tricks while you're telling another
group of friends a ghost story. Below are a few tricks the
first group of friends can help you play. Use your
imagination and come up with ideas of your own.

1. A friend can throw small pebbles against the outside of
   the window of the room you're in. Try and arrange for
   it to happen at a point in your story when you talk
   about a ghost tapping on the window.

2. A friend can shine a torch outside the window at a
   point in your story when you talk about strange lights
   being seen. If the light inside is off, the light being
   shone outside will stand out more.

3. During the day, tie some fishing line to a couple of
   objects in the room where you'll be telling the story.
   During the story, a friend can pull the end of the fishing
   line from under the doorframe or an open window. It
   will appear as if the objects are moving on their own.

4. If you don't have anyone to help you play tricks, you
   can still do it yourself. Use a tape recorder to record
   some scary noises on a audiotape. Set the tape recorder
   up somewhere in the house. Before starting the ghost
   story, press the 'Play' button. You should have about
   fifteen minutes of silence on the audiotape, then the
   strange noises should begin. The scary noises should
   only be heard every now and again.

Number 94:
The Severed Finger

You don't have to play this joke at night. In fact, the fake blood will appear brighter during the day than at night. It's probably best if you don't play this joke on someone with a weak stomach. You may find yourself with a fainting victim.

The Sting

You tell your victim that you have something special to show them. Warn them that it is a little bit scary but don't tell them what it is. You want to give them a big surprise. Show them a matchbox that you have in your hand. Hold the matchbox in front of their face. Push the matchbox tray out towards them, but not all of the way out. When the victim looks inside, they see a severed finger soaked in blood. They scream and faint.

What You Need

- a matchbox

- a pair of scissors

- cotton wool

- tomato sauce (or something else that looks like blood)

The Set-up

1. Get a matchbox.

2. Take out the matches.

3. Using the scissors, cut off one end of the matchbox tray.

4. Place some cotton wool in the tray. The cotton wool makes the finger look like a proper exhibit from a crime scene.

5. Pour some of the fake blood on the cotton wool.

6. Just before playing the joke, put one of your fingers through the tray so that it is sitting on top of the cotton wool. You can add a little more fake blood if you want, this time on top of your finger.

7. Approach the victim and tell them you have something to show them.

8. Show them the 'severed' finger. If they don't faint, tell them a story about where you found the finger or who it came from. Make the story as scary as possible.

Number 95: Bless You

This isn't so much a scary joke as a sick joke. It is great to play on someone when you are waiting in a queue. Try it next time you're standing in line at the school canteen.

The Sting

The victim is standing in a queue. They are waiting patiently to be served. Suddenly the person behind them sneezes and the victim's neck is hit by wet spray.

What You Need

- a water pistol
- some water
- a queue of people

The Set-up

1. Put some water into the water pistol.

2. Find a queue of people. It could be at a bus stop, the school canteen or at a cinema box office.

3. Pull out your water pistol, but don't let anyone see it.

4. Pretend to sneeze. Make it as loud as you can.

5. At exactly the same time as you sneeze, squirt a little bit of water onto the neck of the person in front of you.

6. Quickly put the water pistol away before they turn around.

7. Pull a hanky out of your pocket. When the victim turns around, you should be blowing your nose in your hanky. Apologise to the victim.

Follow-up

- If you want to disgust your victim further, offer to wipe their neck with your hanky. Hold your hanky out to them so that they see small, green chunks fall out of it. Make the chunks from the inside of a grape. Just peel the skin off a grape, pull the seeds out and cut the rest into small chunks. Place the chunks in your hanky. If this doesn't make your victim feel sick, nothing will.

Number 96: Sore Neck

Like the Bless You practical joke, Sore Neck is not really scary but it will make people feel pretty sick. The success of this joke depends a great deal on your ability as an actor.

The Sting

You are sitting next to your victim. You complain that you have a sore neck. A few minutes later, you complain again. This time, you ask the victim to gently massage the back of your neck. The victim does, but the massage doesn't seem to do any good. A couple of minutes later, you grab your head and turn it sharply to the side. The movement is accompanied by a loud cracking sound that makes the victim cry out. You simply shake your head a couple of times and smile, as if you feel much better.

What You Need

- a plastic cup

The Set-up

Gee! That crunching neck of yours sounds like a plastic cup being squashed! You should get it seen to!

CRUNCH

1. This joke works best on a long bus trip.

2. Make sure you are sitting next to your victim.

3. After a while, complain about having a sore neck and shake it from side to side a couple of times. (Do this gently, you don't really want to hurt your neck.)

4. A few minutes later, complain that your neck is still sore and ask the victim to give your neck a quick massage. It

doesn't really matter if the victim agrees to massage your neck or not. It's just a good way to mention your neck again and build up the joke.

5. A few minutes later, complain again about your neck. Tell the victim that you're going to try to snap your neck back into place.

6. Without the victim seeing, place the plastic cup between your body and upper arm.

7. Grab your head with both hands. Breathe heavily a few times as if you are bracing yourself for something painful.

8. Twist your head to the side, while dropping your arm hard against the plastic cup. The cup should crush and make a loud cracking sound.

9. Sigh in relief, then smile at your victim. They'll probably be as white as a sheet believing that you've cracked the bones in your neck.

10. You should practise the twisting and crushing movement a few times at home, as the timing is very important.

Number 97: Fake UFO

UFO stands for Unidentified Flying Object. They are often referred to as Flying Saucers. Some people believe that UFOs from outer space exist. Other people believe they do not exist. Now it's your turn to try and make people believe that you've seen a UFO.

The Sting

You tell a few people that you saw a UFO. Most of them do not believe you. You tell them over and over again you saw a UFO. Still they do not believe you. You take them to the place where the UFO landed. The grass certainly has some strange marks on it. Some of them still require convincing. Imagine their shock and surprise when you produce photos that you took of the UFO. The proof is in front of their eyes.

What You Need

- a lawn mower or grass cutters
- dark shoe polish
- a camera
- a plate or frisbee
- a torch
- someone to help

The Set-up

1. Ask your friends if any of them saw strange lights in the sky the night before.

2. The following day, tell your friends that you saw strange lights in the sky again.

3. Go to an area where there is a large patch of grass, such as a local park.

4. Use the lawn mower or grass cutters to cut a patch of grass into a particular shape, such as a star or circle.

5. Use the shoe polish to make marks that look like burn marks.

6. The following day, tell your friends that you saw more strange lights the night before and followed them. Tell your friends that you saw a UFO land in the park.

7. Your friends will probably not believe that you saw a UFO, so offer to take them to the park.

8. Take them to the park and show them the burn marks you made. Some of your friends may believe you now, but others will need more convincing.

9. Later that day, when it gets dark, go outside with a friend who's in on the joke. Take the camera, the torch and the plate or frisbee.

10. Get your friend to throw the plate or frisbee in the air and shine the torch towards it. While this is happening, take a photo of the plate or frisbee. Repeat this several times.

That's no flying saucer...! That's one of your Mum's old dinner plates!

No way! Look closer.' That's no dinner plate! That's a spaceship from another world! I took the photos myself in our backyard!

11. Get the photos developed. At least one of them should look a bit like a UFO with an eerie light behind it.

12. Next time you see your friends, tell them that you followed the UFO the night before and this time you took a photo. Then show them the photo as proof.

Number 98: Feeling Sick

If this joke doesn't make the person sitting next to you feel sick, then there's something very wrong with them. It's a great joke to play on plane and bus trips.

The Sting

The victim is on a long bus trip. They just want the trip to be over. Suddenly, the person sitting next to them grabs a

paper bag and vomits into it. They then wipe their face and lean back, holding onto the bag. A few minutes later, the sick person appears to be feeling better. The victim looks on with shock and disgust as the sick person grabs a spoon, opens the bag and begins to eat the contents.

What You Need

- a paper bag

- a can of creamed corn (or other chunky food stuff)

- a spoon

The Set-up

1. Before the bus or plane trip begins, or when your victim is away from their seat, tip the contents of the can into the paper bag.

2. At some point in the trip, mention to the victim that you are feeling a bit sick.

3. A few minutes later, moan a little bit.

4. A few minutes later, grab the paper bag, lurch forward in your seat and pretend to vomit into the bag.

5. Sit back and wipe your mouth.

6. A few minutes later, apologise to the victim and tell them you are feeling better.

7. Grab a spoon, open the bag and begin to eat the contents.

8. If you want to gross the victim out even more, offer them a spoonful.

Fake Celebrity Jokes

The practical jokes in this chapter are designed to embarrass or trick friends in public. Some friends, however, may really enjoy having these jokes played on them because for a few minutes they will experience life as a celebrity.

Number 99: Mobbing a Celebrity

This joke requires the help of a number of people all acting out parts. It is quite an elaborate trick, but it is great fun. It can be carried out at an airport, or at any other public place, such as a shopping centre.

The Sting

Your friend is in a public place. Suddenly, your friend is surrounded by a group of people with cameras and notepads. They seem to be journalists. The journalists shout questions at your friend, such as 'Tell us how it felt to win the Academy Award' or 'What's it like to score the match-winning goal?'. Your friend wonders what is going on, but the questions continue and the journalists follow your friend for some time. Members of the public try to catch a glimpse of your friend, whom they assume is a major celebrity.

What You Need

- pretend journalists and photographers

- cameras with flashes

- notebooks and pens

The Set-up

1. Brief the actors so that they know what role they have to play and what questions they have to ask the victim.

2. Give the actors their props and get them to stand in position.

3. Indicate to the actors who the victim is, then give them the signal to start the joke.

4. The joke ends when one of the actors calls out a key word that all the others have been told to listen for. As soon as this word is shouted out, everybody runs away, leaving your friend wondering what's going on.

5. When the actors have run away, leaving the victim bewildered, you can come out from where you've been hiding and observing the joke. Approach the victim with a grin on your face.

Set-up Tips

- The people playing the joke should be old enough to pass themselves off as professional journalists and photographers.

- Your friend should not know any of the people playing the joke.

- Make sure that the questions the journalists ask are consistent. That means you have to decide what sort of celebrity you are going to make your friend.

- Make sure that the journalists keep shouting questions, one after the other. They should ignore claims by your friend that they are not really a celebrity.

Number 100: Mobbing a Pop Star

This joke is similar to Mobbing a Celebrity, except that the people you use to help play the joke can be younger.

The Sting

Your friend is in a public place. Suddenly, a group of young boys and girls mob your friend. They are screaming and hysterical. They want autographs and they want to touch and kiss your friend. The boys and girls are acting as if your friend is the world's greatest pop star. Your friend wonders what's going on and is very embarrassed. Members of the public try to catch a glimpse of your friend, whom they assume is a major pop star.

What You Need

- a group of willing, screaming people

- autograph books and pens

- specially made-up CDs

The Set-up

1. Brief the actors so that they know what role they have to play and what questions they have to ask the victim.

2. Give the actors their props and get them to stand in position.

3. Indicate to the actors who the victim is, then give them the signal to start the joke.

4. The joke ends when one of the actors calls out a key word that all the others have been told to listen for. As soon as this word is shouted out, everybody runs away, leaving your friend wondering what's going on.

5. When the actors have run away, leaving the victim bewildered, you can come out from where you've been hiding and observing the joke. Approach the victim with a grin on your face.

Set-up Tips

- The people posing as screaming fans should not be known to your friend.

- Make sure that the fans keep screaming and asking for autographs. They should ignore claims by your friend that they are not really a pop star.

- To make the situation appear even more convincing, have some of the fans hold CDs with a picture of your friend on the cover.

Number 101:
The Waiting Limo

This trick takes place at an airport, when your friend has just returned from a holiday. If your friend's parents are also at the airport, you should let them know beforehand what you have planned. Otherwise they may step in and ruin the joke.

The Sting

Your friend returns home from an interstate holiday. They get off the plane and start walking through the departure tunnel towards the airport Arrivals lounge. In the lounge,

they see a uniformed chauffeur holding a sign with their name on it. Your friend tells the chauffeur that that's their name. The chauffeur welcomes your friend home and says a limousine is awaiting them outside. The chauffeur carries your friend's bags out of the airport and around the corner, where there is nothing but a bicycle. The look on your friend's face is priceless.

What You Need

- a bicycle
- a piece of cardboard with your friend's name written on it
- a chauffeur's uniform
- a grown-up person your friend doesn't know (to act as the chauffeur)

The Set-up

1. Before the victim even goes on holiday, inform the victim's parents of the joke you are going to play.

2. Choose an adult the victim does not know to act as the chauffeur.

3. Dress the adult in a chauffeur's uniform.

4. Find out which flight the victim is arriving on.

5. Write the victim's name on a piece of cardboard.

6. Go to the airport with the chauffeur.

7. Position the chauffeur in a prominent place and make sure they are holding the sign up high.

8. Position the bicycle around the corner and get someone to watch it so that it is not stolen (or keep an eye on it yourself).

9. Wait for the fun.

Set-up Tips

- It is vital that the victim sees the chauffeur. Position the chauffeur at the Arrivals lounge or at the bottom of the escalators leading to the baggage collection point.

- Another way to make sure that your friend does not miss the chauffeur is for the chauffeur to follow your friend, from a distance, as soon as your friend gets off the plane. When your friend picks up their baggage, the chauffeur will be standing close by, holding the sign up.

- If your friend is suspicious and does not want to follow the chauffeur, have the chauffeur tell them that the limousine trip is a gift from you, or someone else they know.